BROOKLYN JOE AND SAL

Two Bensonhurst Boys

A TRIBUTE TO SALVATORE LA PUMA
AND OUR NEIGHBORHOOD

JOSEPH C. POLACCO

For information regarding permission, please write to: info@barringerpublishing.com
Barringer Publishing, Naples, Florida
www.barringerpublishing.com

Cover and layout by Linda S. Duider

ISBN: 978-1-954396-41-8
Library of Congress Cataloging-in-Publication Data
Brooklyn Joe and Sal: Two Bensonhurst Boys / Joseph C. Polacco

Printed in U.S.A.

To:

Laura

Joseph

Ben

Tess

Linda

Cobi

Miles

Luca

And to Nancy, and her
beautiful family, which is
mine as well

86th Street in the old days (early '50s). The Williamsburg bank branch on the corner of 23rd Avenue looked like the Taj Mahal peering over the teeming, mostly immigrant mix on 86th Street, as if a tropical flower pushed up through the rich loam of the 'hood.

CONTENTS

BROOKLYN JOE AND SAL
A TRIBUTE TO SALVATORE LA PUMA AND OUR BENSONHURST NEIGHBORHOOD

Vinnie, Face and Voice of Bensonhurst. Vinnie was a fixture under the West End el on the NE corner of Bay Parkway and 86th Street. Vinnie was not homeless; it is said his father dropped him off in the morning and took him home in the evening. I'm sure the neighborhood merchants (and denizens like Mamma) made sure he wasn't hungry, and had access to sanitary facilities.

Bensonhurst to a Tee. Vinnie's spot is just under the young lady's left shoulder. The hallowed corner of Bay 31st and 86th Streets (my corner) is indicated by (*). Turn East on that corner to view the full glory of the Casbah market on page vi.

PREFACE

A tribute to Salvatore La Puma
and our neighborhood.

I love his name, so operatic, and yet so Brooklyn. Salvatore La Puma (1929–2008) received the Flannery O'Connor Short Fiction Award for *The Boys of Bensonhurst* (University of Georgia Press, 1987). I was born in Brooklyn's Bensonhurst neighborhood fifteen years after Mr. La Puma and stayed until leaving for college though Bensonhurst and I never parted ways. Bensonhurst breeds stories, which I usually exchange with *paesani, landsmen*, and ex-pats in general from the old neighborhood. Mr. La Puma's stories were "fictional." Mine are recollections, to the extent that my recall is reliable, complete, and unbiased (fat chance). With this collection, my aim is to outline *some* of the influences on this Italian kid born near the end of World War II. Multiethnic inputs imprinted me from the start at the Bensonhurst Maternity Hospital across from the Jewish Community House on Bay Parkway and 79th Street. JCH activities kept Mamma awake, as if I needed help.

On my first birthday, July 16, 1945, America detonated the first atomic bomb in Los Alamos, New Mexico. Three weeks later, World War II was effectively over when we unleashed an A-bomb on Hiroshima, putting me on the cusp of the postwar baby boom. Twenty-one years after Los Alamos, I had been a college graduate for a whole month. That Bachelor of Science did not turn this Bensonhurst boy to a man. Rather, it was a road marker in my exploration of the internal and external influences I experienced when I moved out of Bensonhurst—which still leaves its mark on my life.

Immigrants entered Bensonhurst from the *shtetls* and ghettos of Eastern Europe or from Southern Italian slums and hardscrabble villages. But mostly they came from stops on generic Delancey Streets and each Little Italy of Manhattan. Bensonhurst was a rung on the ladder to the American dream.

Bensonhurst is romanticized in popular culture. It is the neighborhood of Jackie Gleason's Ralph Kramden in TV's *The Honeymooners* (1955), of the elevated train chase in *The French Connection* (William Friedkin, director, 1971), of James Buchanan (really, New Utrecht) High of TV's *Welcome Back, Kotter* (1975), and of John Travolta's Tony Manero, the Disco Don of *Saturday Night Fever* (John Badham, director, 1977). By the way, the train in *The French Conection* went by our linoleum store three times. Very few viewers noticed.

For the immigrants of La Puma's stories (1939-1943), Bensonhurst was a meaner place of working-class families, numbers runners, loan sharks, hot and dusty garment sweatshops, social clubs of "guys in fedoras," bookie joints, pool halls, corner bars, and at least one factory that produced counterfeit olive oil. Business protection could be bought from the fedoras, at premiums hard to refuse.

But my Bensonhurst and La Puma's also had rooftop pigeon coops for hobbyists, heavenly pastry shops (*pasticerrie*), bakeries, and pizzerias, often combined into one, and within walking distance. Among others: DeFilippi, Reliable, and Mondiale. Other shops specialized in bagels, *bialys,* and onion boards. I was often sent across 86th Street to pick up rye bread and *challah* from Schlom and Deutch Bakery. And 86th Street still features open-air markets where you can bargain for fresh artichokes, buy a live eel, or be serenaded by frustrated tenors. People sat on evening summer stoops variously enjoying Italian ices, Dr. Brown's Cel-Ray soda, a pastrami on rye, whatever, while the kids played sidewalk games or street stickball. All were welcome to summertime parish street festivals featuring songs from the old country, dollar bill-robed saints in procession, games of chance, and incredible food. Family ties were strong over the years of La Puma's stories, before and during World War II, and just before I came on the scene. They were still strong when I left for graduate school in summer 1966.

Two years after La Puma's 1987 book, Bensonhurst gained notoriety as the neighborhood of the killer(s) of young Black Yusuf Hawkins. The Hawkins incident became an Italian versus Black *cause célèbre*, and that especially hurts. Then again, I look at the camaraderie of the multiracial high school athletic teams of Lincoln and New Utrecht. There is always hope.

Mamma visited a Bensonhurst march organized by Reverend Al Sharpton in support of justice for Hawkins. She offered a "peace" button to a marching lady, uttering "peace" with the gesture. The lady looked at Mamma and the button, and responded with "F—— peace, I want war." Ensued an intemperate response by Mamma which she regretted the rest of her life.

Michael Grandé Polacco, my musician brother, had a colleague, Bruce Johnson, who lived in a Black enclave at the south end of very Italian 18th Ave. Bruce was a superb jazz guitarist and the son of Austin Johnson of the Ink Spots, nationally popular vocal group of the '30s and '40s. Bruce was the last Bensonhurst acquaintance I encountered en route to La Guardia Airport, and thence to grad school at Duke University. The chance meeting took place late summer 1966 over hot dogs and crinkle-cut fries at Nathan's Famous in Coney Island. Bruce gave me both a hearty greeting and a warm send-off to the postgraduate "man-child phase" of my life.

Bensonhurst today has a few dwindling and shrinking Italian enclaves, surrounded by people of other ethnicities, mainly Chinese. Change happens, and people always decry the new residents. (I must say that many *paesani* who couldn't wait to flee Bensonhurst now fill Facebook pages pining over the lost treasure of the good old days.) Seymour W, a Jewish buddy of my stepfather, told me that "only the last names change, but it's still the same complaint" about the next immigrant wave. True, perhaps, but skin color and Asian features are more indelible than accents, or names that can be hyphenated or anglicized. And Stepdad's same friend also defended the very large families of Orthodox Jews: "They're saving the white race." At the time, I did not fully appreciate that Seymour implied the danger of *replacement*.

The concept of replacement of whites is now lodged in my ageing brain. On a recent visit to Manhattan, I loved seeing Black and Latino help at Katz's Deli on Houston Street and at Kossar's Bagels/Bialys on Grand. Not only the staff but the clientele was multicolored. If this is replacement, bring it on. May the ranks of the owners as well acquire new colors and accents. And, duhhh, . . . my white cousins (can I get a familial embrace?): Don't keep reducing each other's ranks, as in the Napoleonic Wars, WWI, WWII, Russia-Ukraine, and other blood baths. Stay home, already, warm the conjugal bed.

Haarlem and *Niew Amsterdam/New York* reflect New York's Dutch and English origins. May that history not diminish those indigenous cultures that occupied the coastal North Atlantic thousands of years before European immigrant "explorers" such as John Cabot (née Giovanni Caboto), Henry Hudson, and Giovanni da Verrazzano visited their eponymous coastal waterways. The etymology of Bensonhurst is more prosaic—in the late 19th

century it was named after developer Arthur Benson, president of Brooklyn Gas Light Company.

We Bensonhurst citizens don't like to acknowledge Bath Beach, the approximately five-avenue strip between Gravesend Bay and Bensonhurst's major business thoroughfare, 86th Street. Some of La Puma's scenes were on the Bath Beach waterfront. The Bensonhurst–Bath Beach boundary line may run through the middle of 86th, putting much of my youth in Bath Beach. *OK, OK, so who's doin' a soivey?* as they probably still say in the neighborhood. And both sides of 86th have the same 11214 zip code, so there.

Bensonhurst was my launch pad and is still my ground control, offering a perspective throughout my life's trajectory. As you travel along with my Bensonhurst and post-Bensonhurst adventures, you will come to know those perspectives too.

I hope the late Mr. La Puma would have agreed that I at least partially stayed on course.

PART I

This Boy of Bensonhurst

(1944 to 1966)

I really was a boy but a mother's love, a supportive stepfather, and lady luck got me through boyhood. And, I learned and matured along the way.

1956: Harbingers of End Times. Sure, Brooklyn won it all in '55, but in '56, Yankees fans scorned us with the retro battle cry, *"Wait'll* **Last** *Year!"* In '56 dem aging Bums squeezed out a last pennant only to see their hitting wane almost to absolute zero in the Series. We scored one run in the last 28 innings.

- Don Larsen (Don Larsen!?) threw a perfect game five.
- We got blasted 9-0 in game seven, at Ebbets!!

Brooklyn finished third in '57, a sign of the Last Days: The erstwhile Bums went from '58 LA Coliseum laughing stocks to winning it all in '59.

We waited 67 years, Angelenos got impatient at two.

Oisk and Sal pitched no-hit gems in '56, heroic resistance to O'Malley's treachery.

Chapter One

• • •

The Witnesses, Part 1
EVOLUTION, BASEBALL, AND THE NEW WORLD
(ca. 1954–1962)

> Is there a single pathway to the Truth?
> Via blind faith or open-eyed science?
> May both ways converge for this youth
> Seeking to forge a feasible alliance

Salvatore La Puma grew up in a very Italian pocket of Bensonhurst and wrote much of young people's relationship with the Catholic Church. I came along fifteen years after Mr. La Puma, and that short generation time marked some differences between us. Yes, I am Italian American, and my neighborhood overall was roughly equal parts Italian and Jewish. Italian meant Catholic, and Jewish, *oy vey*, usually meant Reformed. We certainly mixed, and intermarried, as also occurred in La Puma's Bensonhurst. Some of the most "flamboyant" young people of my boyhood were products of such mixed marriages. I don't ascribe flamboyance to hybrid vigor, perhaps more to stimulation in a mixed-culture home environment. As a geneticist, I often faced the G x E conundrum—Genetic versus Environmental influences on gene expression. In Bensonhurst, some could be convinced that G x E was *goy* x *eshkenazi*.

Italians and Jews both believe in family, and food. In my boyhood, Italians were more likely to grow produce in front and back yards: eggplants, tomatoes, basil (*basilicò*), calabash (*cucuzza*, or goo-gootz in street slang), etc. Many *paesani* produced their own figs and wine, and backyard chickens and rooftop pigeon coops could provide animal protein. Jews tended to live in apartments in larger buildings though over the years Jews as well became enlightened urban farmers.

My aim is not to distinguish Ashkenazi/Eshkenazi Jews from Southern Italians, but rather to distinguish my religious youth from that portrayed by Mr. La Puma. Salvatore's local Catholic parish was more than a meeting place for Sunday Mass, it was a community center, and the effigies spoke to the faithful. In *The Jilted Groom [1940]*,[1] young Vito Conti could hear the wooden Christ on His cross *kvetching*/complaining in His "Sicilian hoarseness" about the church's cold air, and how He could have been somebody back in the old country. (The soliloquy itself is worth the price of the book, and it could have been uttered about America in general by the hood's ancient immigrants who mixed benediction and blasphemy.)

I lost out on these ecclesiastical connections: In my preadolescence, I was steered away from the Catholic Church. I became a Jehovah's Witness. I have not confessed this to many.

---

[1] References to La Puma's Bensonhurst stories are given by *Chapter Title [story year]*.

4

Back then, I feared that the *deep Vatican State* would know of my wayward ways. Now, I am screaming them to my readership, limited though it may be.

The Witnesses of Brooklyn were laudable in that they "co-housed" Italians, Jews, and people of all other races and colors. Yet, within that house, I had my own private room. How was I "steered" into my cell within an organized religion/sect that walled itself off from the world at large? At this distance, I try to order chronological events.

My Sicilian stepfather was probably the conduit. I believe he was a Witness before he entered my life but was "disfellowshipped" under circumstances I can never confirm, and I will not invent possible scenarios. To me, Stepdad was always a good man, tormented by his own mortality. His estranged wife, a neighborhood woman I (thankfully) never met, was a Witness in good standing. The oldest of her four children, Eloisa, for as long as I knew her, was very committed to the religion, self-named *The Truth*. Eloisa's mother remained in The Truth until her passing, well before my mother's 2013 passing.

My first recollection of the Witnesses was Mamma taking me to a meeting in a sparsely appointed hall. This 10/11-year-old had no idea what was going on. I knew no one, and Stepdad was not there. But people were friendly. I was escorted to a few more meetings and then eventually started going on my own. After a couple of years, I found myself a "member." There was no inflection point, no membership card—being in good standing entailed weekly Bible study in a small group at a Witness's home and evening meetings (Thursday and Sunday) in a Kingdom Hall (our spartan "parish"). But our *raison d'être* was door-to-door proselytizing, Saturday and/or Sunday mornings—hence,

"Witnessing." There was pressure to do incidental witnessing in daily life, as in around the office water cooler or in a school locker room.

I tried mightily to avoid incidental witnessing. Door-to-door was scary enough, each opening portal a possible unveiling of my religious affiliation to an acquaintance or relative. Just standing at the threshold in my jacket and tie, with Bible in hand, a satchel of literature, and accompanied by an earnest, beaming colleague, was an eloquent testimony.

Within the Kingdom Hall, experiences were not all negative. For one, the Hall helped my public speaking. I was obliged to read assigned Bible passages to the whole congregation. Later in my development, I presented prepared talks on a biblical passage or an article in the organization's magazines, either *Awake* or *The Watchtower*. The former offered commentary on the sorry state

Another harbinger of end times.

of This World, the latter a more rigorous dissection of biblical passages, especially as they pertained to the "end times." I do not recall females making such presentations, and at the time I did not even think about it. A positive aspect of presenting was that I was obliged to wear a jacket and tie, which occasioned compliments from some of the ladies.

Through all this, I was pretty much a 'Lone Ranger Witness' within my family, though Mamma did attend my presentations and Stepdad always gave me car fare to the Hall. Why did I maintain an association? Difficult to answer: Yes, there was "fellowship," and girls my age were a draw. I think one "hook" was the possibility that the Witnesses might be right, and I had better not waste the opportunity to be saved—better to heed the Word than to hear and then reject It. Older folks, possibly assigned mentors, took an interest in my spiritual development. While we traded observations on baseball, Sputnik, and current events, it was clear I was not to be of that World. I was a rabid Brooklyn Dodgers fan, which was akin to idolatry, and they used that word. I was torn between two worlds.

At the age of thirteen or fourteen I was baptized—immersed in a downtown Brooklyn YMCA pool. I was in a state of astonishment on the lonely subway ride home. Somehow, my kid brother escaped all this internal turmoil.

What have I done? Is there no going back? What will be expected of me now?

Of course, I should have asked those questions before being held under the water. To use Bensonhurst terms, I've always been a little *meshuggeneh*, a *stunad*, a little crazy, too dumb, and too easy. My partner Nancy has told me, more than once, "Good thing you weren't born a girl."

In general, it was not easy for anyone to be a "Witness." Though we lived in This World, we were apart from it. We were law-abiding but refused the draft and did not pledge allegiance—to me a recurring torture as I felt eyes on me during this daily school exercise. Receiving a blood transfusion was a sure way to be denied everlasting life in Jehovah's New World, the earth remade to a paradise wherein the lion lays down with the lamb.

Current events as always seemed to be driving us to Armageddon—the defeat of Satan in the ultimate battle, his casting off from the earth, which was to be transformed into the New World of the righteous, many of whom to be resurrected to eternal life.

My love for baseball clashed with *The Truth*. I played one year on the St. Bernadette parish entry in the Coney Island Grasshopper League for twelve-year-olds. On "opening day" my teammates and I, in our new uniforms, stood on the lawn outside the Knights of Columbus Hall (86th St. and 13th Ave.) for a blessing by the monsignor, perched on a balcony as if a local Pope. Later, came the Babe Ruth and Police Athletic Leagues, and high school teams. I so envied teammates who were encouraged by their parish to play sports. In their world, there was no conflict between baseball and religion. One of my teammates, Morty Ehrlich, was Jewish and no problem there either.

Entering the St. Bernadette League of "organized baseball" was joyous. A couple of buddies and I walked to the parish in Dyker Heights and signed up. I had to return with parental signatures and registration money to make it official, but before making it back to Bensonhurst we were confronted by three local guys our age. Socioeconomically, Dyker Heights was a step or two up from Bensonhurst. That night we defended the honor of Bensonhurst.

One memorable Sunday morning, I had clashing commitments—proselytize door-to-door or play in a Coney Island League game. Satan and Jehovah were on opposite shoulders, and I was inclined to ignore both—when I heard my name coming through my bedroom window. Some teammates and my coach were calling for me from Mr. Spadaro's verdant Sicilian-style vineyard and garden around the block and behind our building. I called out to them from my side of the chain-link fence. That morning I was pushed toward Satan but had a great time playing a good game. And my teammates knew nothing of my religion, or sinning ways.

Mamma never attended a game, and Stepdad never took me to one—I walked, took a bus or subway, or caught a ride with a coach or a teammate's parent to the appointed diamond. Mamma worked every day, in a garment sweatshop or at home where, in addition to housekeeping, she made apparel to order and did alterations.

Stepdad did attend my first awards night, in the St. Bernadette Confraternity Hall, and was in shock when I was awarded our team MVP (and shook hands onstage with Dodgers legends Happy Felton and Gino Cimoli). Stepdad thanked my coaches, but an *Ozzie and Harriet* household we were not. I can't help conjecturing that a 16-year-old Anthony Fauci may have been in the audience that night. He lived on 13th Avenue one block from the parish.

My best buddy, Petey LaMontia, was my first baseball school. We played all year round, just as long as there was no snow, mud or puddles on the dirt infield of the Bensonhurst Park diamond, hard by Trump's Shore Haven Apartments. Our baseballs were often taped up, but we saved up for the joyous occasional purchase of a brand-new ball. It seems now like we spent hours pitching to each other, fielding grounders, or chasing down fungoes. (Petey agrees.)

Then there were other schools: Father Varriale of St. Bernadette was a knowledgeable and driving baseball coach. He advised us to take up catching if we wanted to advance far in baseball. Catching was as close as he got to catechism.

My love for biology clashed with *The Truth*. Evolution was anathema to the Witnesses—a false doctrine. Of course, paraphrasing Theodosius Dobzhansky (an evolutionary biologist/geneticist *and* a devout Christian) biology only makes sense through the lens of evolution, and I was very much into biology. *Awake* used biological discoveries to expound on Jehovah's wonderful creation, but never found any example to buttress evolutionary theory. At the Stuyvesant High School of Science in Lower Manhattan, I became more "of this world," more under Satan's influence. The West End Express took me twice daily over the Manhattan Bridge on my scholarly commute. In each direction, the bridge offered a full view of the Witnesses' Brooklyn-based world headquarters, its neon lights announcing Jehovah's Kingdom. While I stopped heeding their messages, apparently Wall Street, on the Manhattan side of the East River, was alert. "Dead Will Rise" meant that it was worth investing in dead stocks. Ya gotta love capitalist cynicism.

I will always love my mother—an incredibly generous and caring person. But I could not understand why I was the toe she dipped into the waters of the Witnesses. At the time, she and Stepdad had serious issues with the Catholic Church, and none of our family of four had anything to do with it. (And my peers knew, if only because I was the only Italian kid in my class not to bear the forehead smudge on Ash Wednesday.) My mother did have a reawakening, and over the last fifty years of her life she was a devout Catholic and found serious fault with the Witnesses. I accompanied her to Mass in Bensonhurst, in Columbia, Missouri, and in Madrid, Spain.

I had drifted far from The Truth during my three years attending Stuyvesant High School. The epiphany came in college during a freshman botany lecture that featured an amazing real-time video of an onion root cell nucleus undergoing mitosis. *That's it, I'm in. I'm a scientist—my lifestyle for learning "the truth."*

But, end of internal conflict? *What if the Witnesses were right by some quirk in logic? Where would that leave me? And why, far from my Brooklyn home, did I not want to answer the door when they "called?"*

Mamma, about 20, with yours truly. My curly angelic locks darkened, and then fell, a tragedy akin to that of the Roman Empire.

Chapter Two

• • •

The Witnesses, Part 2
DIVINE FAMILY BLISS
(ca. 1958–1962)

> If disquiet and doubt are paths to heaven
> I took furtive steps on that rocky road
> Then sampling a spiritual delicatessen
> I turned to the fasting my vision bestowed

My association with the Jehovah's Witnesses wasn't all pangs of guilt, internal conflict, and embarrassment. Did I mention the girls? And I did have a sports outlet in a good buddy from a family of converts from Judaism. Now, culturally they were very Jewish—almost TV stereotypes. Philip R and family lived in predominantly Jewish Brighton Beach, one beach over from Coney Island. They were well-off. Dad was a Broadway agent of some kind. Sam and his wife had three strapping boys and one beautiful daughter, Naomi. I was buddies with the baby, Philip. *How could Philip manage to live a normal life in very Jewish Brighton?* I'm sure his

Left: **Vina, Jijjie and Ben, 2, 6 and 7 years-old (May 1927).** Vina was meant to be a momma. At two in May 1927, she was already involved in her brothers' imbroglios. She had the genes to rear a middle guard, though I was able to trim down my gams (Chapter 7). The fourth, Angie, had not been born at picture time.

Right: **Mamma in our back-of-store kitchen during my college days, 1962-1966 (and into the mid-70's).** Sure we had three rooms, but they were petite, as was our only kitchen sink (*M. deSade Designs*, Inc.). My back hurts as I look at mamma at the sink.

In truth, we also had a bathroom sink. And the bath tub could serve culinary purposes, such as holding a pot of marine snails, on which the lid was left ajar to let in light, thereby catching the snails peering out, ready to throw into a sauce. After playing with the snails for a while, I once left the lid completely off, obliging us to pull our dinner off bathtub and bathroom walls.

buddies all knew of his family's incompatible religion that, for instance, fervently believed Jesus was the son of God. (Whose name Jehovah, at least, was derived from the Hebrew *Yahweh*.)

I loved visiting with Philip, to play some hoops in a beachfront park or just to hang out. And there were girls, most of them Jewish. A vivid memory is looking into the eyes of a Jewish young lady in front of a jukebox, as she swayed and resonated with the music and lyrics of "Little Star." Now, the song was by the Elegants, five nice Italian boys who gave informal performances under the boardwalk in South Beach, Staten Island (thank you, Wikipedia). "Little Star" came out in 1958, the summer I turned fourteen. So, this very cute Jewish gal was *on* the Brighton boardwalk, making her own cultural connection with doo-wop from *under* another boardwalk. When I think of such weird social and cultural juxtapositions I can only say "what a country!" It sounds better in a Yiddish accent.

Philip and I were on competing teams in a baseball league that played most of its games at the Lincoln High School field in Coney Island. Philip's Jewish coach was gruff and aggressive. His Italian wife was very much his co-coach. She was a spitfire during games. But before and after she always asked me how my hitting was coming along, while choking up on an imaginary bat.

Four young Jehovah's Witnesses (Philip and I plus another Italian, and another youth) worked like animals over several sticky summer days steaming paper off the walls in Philip's apartment. Mr. R rewarded us with good tickets to *West Side Story* at the Winter Garden Theatre. I never would have experienced the show and the Broadway scene if I had stayed within my Bensonhurst circles. Chita Rivera as Anita was amazing. More amazing to me was the well-dressed, out-of-town, WASP audience getting so much into New York City's gang conflicts—to me a forgettable and deplorable aspect of city life.

By the end of my three years at Stuyvesant, my association with the Witnesses was moribund, but I did still hang with Philip. At Brighton Beach just after high school graduation, one of Philip's friends asked how I did on the (New York State) Regents physics exam. My score in the low-90s won respect from both the guys and girls. So, I was not exactly chopped liver. That I was headed to Cornell also held sway, and not once that day did a discussion of religion enter the picture.

The older of Philip's two brothers was a legendary fullback at Lincoln High—another link to This World, this old system of things. But it did provide his bro a measure of respect among the flock. Philip's sister Naomi married a very good-looking and articulate Italian boy, Louis L. She was fair-skinned, a little freckled, with luminous hazel eyes, and just ever so slightly and alluringly *zaftig*. He was, well . . . tall, dark, and handsome (and fluent in two languages). Such a beautiful couple, and I can say that in both Italian and Yiddish intonation. They commandeered the Kingdom Hall to show slides of their European honeymoon. Yet, they became "Pioneers," dedicating their daily lives to announcing Jehovah's Kingdom, proselytizing. I could never have done that, not even with Naomi by my side.

Philip's father, Sam, could be a lovable character, like when he led the congregation in hymns by authoritatively plunking the Hall's piano keys with strong fat fingers, or when he partook of comfort food at the 65th Street Isaac Gellis Delicatessen, two doors away from the stairway to the Kingdom Hall. *Après* dinner, he'd take his place in the back of the audience, usually between two unoccupied folding chairs, and variously emanate *eau de* mustard, sauerkraut, knish, kreplach, all-beef kosher hot dog, and other delicacies.

But Sam also showed a stern side. Philip's mom had given her son fifty cents before he left for the beach one day, and he responded with "Oh rhapsody!" Such typical Jewish sarcasm was not appreciated. We were seated for lunch, and Sam was about to say grace. Philip looked over at his bearish dad and impatiently uttered, "Well?" to which Mrs. R grabbed Philip while Dad pulled off his own belt. He gave Philip a thrashing that brought proud son to tears. I feared for my own well-being but came through unscathed. That day I learned of Philip's resentment against both parents.

You don't have to be Italian, or Catholic, to come from a stressful home environment. I learned that before college—AP (Advanced Placement) credit for sure.

In La Puma's *Gravesend Bay [1940]*, Mario chided his Sicilian wife for going so much to confession with Father Hartigan.

"What's an Irishman know about Sicilian sins?"

To me, the Witnesses were much more ecumenical than the Catholic Church—all races and religions were thrown together in our minestrone of moral misery. We were bonded by sin and doubt. But I could not reconcile their faith with my "objective" belief structure. Then again, as an agnostic I ask, who knows the real Truth?

Above: **Mamma and Stepdad Lou** (second and third from right, seated) **at the Bensonhurst Board of Trade Dance, Oriental Manor, Oct. 1978.** Lou was definitely in his sartorial phase, and Mamma was wearing an elegant dress of her own design and fabrication. Not sure if snails were on the menu. Note the halo over stepdad's coif. Seymour W. is to Stepdad's right.

Below: **Grandpa's linoleum store (1982).** With his three grandkids Laura, Benji, and Joseph. Note the ornate Doric and Corinthian columns.

Chapter Three

• • •

A STROLL THROUGH THE PARK
(ca. 1961)

While walking along a bucolic path
I was met by some angry young people
Could I assuage their strident wrath
With words of wisdom, in no way feeble?
 Later I asked, what provokes such rage?
Do the youngsters read rejection and hate
In those who won't share the stage
But rather cast scorn and incriminate?

 Caminando por un sendero bucólico
Me encontré con rabiosos mozalbetes
Manteniendo mi balance armónico
Sobreviví con gestos de un Manolete
 Luego me pregunté ¿por qué tanta rabia?
¿Sienten los jóvenes rechazo y enemistad?
Y en lugar de tomar la dulce savia
¿Aguantan golpes amargos a su dignidad?

Throughout high school, my Bensonhurst home was those three rooms behind our linoleum store on the south side of busy 86th Street—between 22nd (Bay Parkway) and 23rd Avenues. That stretch was a warren of delis, food shops, outdoor and indoor produce, and *chachka* stands. It sounded and smelled like a casbah. Adding to the cacophony, the West End line ran above it. From the Bay Parkway station, the train went to Coney Island Beach in three stops (and three more on the Brighton Beach line to Philip R's place). The other direction was labeled "To City," to the wonders of Manhattan. Don't cry for me; I felt privileged in either direction.

One of the Manhattan wonders was the Stuyvesant High School of Science, and my attendance there made me a nerd in Bensonhurst, at least on the street, which was roughly split between Italians and Jews, equal opportunity tough guys who often engaged in wise guy ("wink") collaborations—loan sharking, bookmaking, etc. There was a smattering of Latinos, Black folks, even some Irish, who seemed exotic to me. I survived because I was a halfway decent athlete, and I did not back down from a fight (and was usually on the verge of going berserk). Luckily, we young people didn't use guns. The closest we came were zip guns, which are another story (see Chapter Nine).

My first language was probably Italian because as a babe I communicated with my caregiving grandmother in her Neapolitan dialect, at least my mother told me so. I don't remember those very early days, but some linguistic trolley grooves must have been laid down. On those tracks, I was able to launch a passable fluency in Spanish, greatly aided by rigorous language training at Stuyvesant, and by a Dominican family who moved into an apartment a block from us on our side of 86th. They were refugees from the turmoil following the assassination of dictator Generalísimo Trujillo. The family had daughters.

Did I say I was a nerd? One summer day, I corralled my kid bro to go on a nature trip, by train. Michael reluctantly agreed. He was disenchanted with school, chafing at following the academic success of his older brother. (We learned later that Michael was dyslexic. However, he communicated beautifully through his music, via his voice, guitar, songwriting, and poetic lyrics.) We got off at lovely, bucolic Central Park West and West 81st Street and climbed stone stairs to the American Museum of Natural History. It was palatial, as if a relic of Manhattan Brahmans of a time gone by. I loved the museum for the obvious reasons of the dinosaurs and dioramas. And admission was minimal back then. But the real lures for me were the huge collections of butterflies and beetles on public display, not locked in storage for research purposes, as they are now.

I was suspended in time, mesmerized by the bugs while Michael showed much forbearance. When we finally left the building, my poor kid brother needed to clear his head, so we crossed the street and strolled through Central Park. We took a turn on a lovely pastoral path and came upon a group of young Latinos, and in those days that meant Puerto Ricans—recall *West Side Story*. They were giving us mean looks. One of the guys at a water fountain very dexterously directed a long stream of water at me. Direct hit. I gave him a mean look back. After all, I was from Bensonhurst and honor was currency anywhere: The code is not to back down, even when not on your own turf. Sal La Puma would have understood.

"Looks like a *faggot* [FAHY-gut] ta me," one of the guys announced. Faggot had morphed from *fag* in those days, but I was not about to give a discourse on divergent etymologies.

Now, brother still claims, sixty-plus years later, that I had turned to tell him not to say a word. Understand that my brother looks more like a gringo than I do. Michael has light hair, clear eyes, and fairer skin. I could pass for Latino, especially in those days and in my summer Coney Island tan. And I was buff, keeping in shape for high school football, so maybe a little threatening but woefully outnumbered.

The guys encircled me. And I was so glad Michael never said we were looking at pretty butterflies and exotic beetles across the street. Michael was completely *mum*, bless his heart.

"Why you give me hard looks?" said the aqueous artillery engineer.

El Señor "Faggot" was almost salivating.

"You got me wet, and I didn't do anything to you." (*Me mojaste, y no te hice nada.*)

The anger in my voice needed no linguistic interpretation. Then the decompression mode kicked in. Cousin Jim Mangano said that growing up in Bensonhurst taught him how to fight, yes, but more importantly, it taught him how to talk. And this *tawk* usually accompanied a beautiful minuet of posturing and strutting.

"Compadres, why you want to mess with me? I'm just trying to do my job, watching this kid for a gringo family."

They looked over at Michael and I went on. "He's a little retarded. He can't speak much in any language."

My turn to look over at Michael. He had that genuine open-mouth, wide-eyed confused look. They seemed to believe me.

One of the guys asked me where I was from. I said, "*De la Isla.*" I exclaimed *Puerto Rico*, "The Island."

He retorted, "Yeah, me too." And then, "From where?"

"Santurce!" I said. I figured they were all from San Juan or another large city, and I knew that Santurce had a baseball team (and a good one) and that it was on the coast 'cause the team was called "The Crabbers" (*Los Cangrejeros*).

Luckily, no one called me on it. I complained about New York, America. Whatever, we BS'd a bunch in bad Spanish and worse English and they musta thought I was an alright guy.

Mr. Faggot gave Michael little pokes. I stepped in between. "*Cuidado, 'mano!* I gotta deliver this guy in one piece," I said with a smile.

We said our goodbyes. Michael and I headed out of the park and to the subway. Bada bing—we got back to the back of the store. There was Mamma home from her sweatshop job, cooking a beautiful aromatic sauce—it was Thursday, pasta night.

"Where'd you go?" she asked.

Michael was still in his mute mode. I offered, "Ahh, we went into New York, to the museum."

"That's nice. What else did you do?" she said, stirring the sauce.

Michael and I looked at each other and uttered a synchronized "nuthin."

Mamma and the mammas of La Puma's Bensonhurst a generation before were happy to see their kids at home, healthy and unmarked. They learned not to ask too many questions, though back in the day, the 'hood collectively seemed to know more than the police about gang and fedora activities.

I knew, and knew of, Michael's friends on the Gravesend waterfront Rampers—Sammy the Bull, Jimmy Emma, Gerard Papa et *al*. These guys were almost a "farm team" to the fedora professionals and few of them had good endings. (Some details are in *Vina, A Brooklyn Memoir* [Joseph C. Polacco, 2016], and the story starts under the 79th Street station of the West End.)

Michael was able to turn away from the Rampers to his music and to high school football because of his mamma and a junior high principal who believed in him.

Benzer and Sagan

Two Bensonhurst Poles:
from the gene to the cosmos

Each Pole (well, one a Ukrainian) escaped Hitler's scythe
As the horned Führer sought to rid Europe of invasive weeds.
In Bensonhurst, 'hood of our refuge, each bloomed at his pole

New Utrecht High's **Seymour Benzer,** physicist who saw the light,
Applied galactic large numbers to bacterial virus
His universe, telescoped down to the petri dish,
Codified units of the gene: structure, size, function
An acolyte, I spouted his new poetry: *recon, muton, cistron*.

For Landsman **Carl Sagan** the cosmos was his petri dish
Not with universal hubris, but boundless humility
In a modest Bensonhurst house he pondered the universe's edges
Their stars legion as celestial viruses, releasing
Boundless imaginations of young space voyagers
    I was part of his quarry.

Chapter Four

. . .

MURL
(1959–1961)

> Rivers, the life blood of civilization
> Bring goods and folks from distant places
> For East River's immigrant sons, an oration:
> Play tough, under Uncle Sam's good graces

I went out for football at Manhattan's Stuyvesant High School.

La Puma wrote of track and cross-country at Bensonhurst's New Utrecht High School (*Gravesend Bay [1940]*). One of his trackmen was Carmine—my middle name because my birthday falls on Our Lady of Mount Carmel day. I thought Sal went too far with Carmine's Carmellini surname, but this is a tribute, not a critique.

La Puma didn't have much truck for football. For me, this was a major omission, since New Utrecht was a football powerhouse and an example of Italian-Jewish convergence. Legendary coach, Sy Rapp, led the mostly Italian American Utes. The Thanksgiving

Seated: Karle, Weinstein, Lichtenstein, Mr. Thrush, Belsky, Freundlich, Nabor, Polacco.

2nd Row: Ungar, Friedman, Zimmerman, Richards, Feinstat, Brendel, Lifson, Johnson, Sachs, Coppa, Adelson, Yamaoka, Dix.

3rd Row: Chernoble, Solomon, Erich, Thustee, Terzuola, Osikowicz, Carol, Tosch, Katz, Markman, Mariotti, Feldman, Pearl.

Not-quite defaced photo of the Stuyvesant HS 1961 football team. While we did not keep the yearbook photo inviolate, at least defensive back Wade Johnson took pains not to run a line through a teammate's face. Though he signed my yearbook and not *Gary Markman's* (with "Here's hoping you attain your goals"), Wade was definitely directionally astute in the defensive backfield.

NOTE ALSO:
- Coach Thrush, the SOLE member of the coaching staff, present and accounted for.
- The catchy white socks.
- The dynamic chevron of my eyebrows: "you lookin' at ME?"

Day game with archrival Lafayette, my neighborhood high school, was dubbed the "Lasagna Bowl" by local pundits. Lafayette was once coached by Sam Rutigliano, who went on to coach the original NFL Cleveland Browns, taking them to the 1980 AFC Championship game—which they lost to the eventual Super Bowl champs, the Oakland Raiders of Brooklyn's Al Davis. The Raiders were led by the first Latino NFL head coach, Tom Flores. Way to go, Al.[2]

Brooklyn's HS football hotbed featured other Jewish-Italian interactions. Erasmus High, a huge school in Flatbush, produced pro football pioneer Al ("Just win, baby") Davis, yes, and going back to the years of La Puma's stories, Sid Luckman. Sid quarterbacked the Chicago Bears (1939–1950) and still holds the NFL career record for touchdowns per pass attempt. (Jewish Luckman played college football at Columbia U under Luigi Piccolo, better known as the anglicized Lou Little.)

How could Stuyvesant, crammed into Manhattan's crowded Lower East Side, even hope to compete with the likes of Lafayette, New Utrecht, and Erasmus? Stuyvesant had no football field, no field of any kind. I had no football experience except for some two-hand touch in the neighborhood streets and on the PS 101 schoolyard concrete. Stuyvesant and I were made for each other.

How could we compete? We had Coach Murl Thrush, an Oklahoma boy who wrestled and played center at Columbia University. (He was also recruited to coach wrestling at the NY Athletic Club and helped establish wrestling programs in NYC high schools.) Then Murl took the Stuyvesant challenge. I emphasize that this is purely my own theory: Murl took the

---

[2] An "older Brother" at my local gym reminded me that Davis also hired the first Black NFL head coach, Art Shell.

football reins at Stuyvesant to atone, in part, for the antisemitic policies of the NYAC.

Not even Stuyvesant's bright student body fully appreciated obstacles Murl had to overcome for football success at our school. First, many Stuyvesantians were "SP," meaning they skipped a grade, thus entering high school lacking a year of physical maturation compared to those at the exalted outer borough powerhouses, and this included our traditional rival, Bronx's DeWitt Clinton High School of five thousand boys. Second, our own numbers, officially half of Clinton's, were effectively smaller because many, if not most of us, entered high school as sophomores, thus losing a year of preparation. I did not play a facsimile of football until the spring of my sophomore year and had never "put the pads on" until late summer before junior year.

Most of us juniors spent the fall season on the bench, and as scrimmage fodder for our seniors. Senior year was my chance at the golden ring.

I went on to play in college, so I appreciate the resources available to college coaches. But show me a head coach at *any* level who taped ankles, led calisthenics and grass drills, and who was so into offensive alignments he had an inches-thick stack of index cards full of X's and O's, arrows, pass routes, downfield blocks, options—they were reminiscent of subatomic particle paths in a cloud chamber, something Stuyvesant guys could appreciate. We'd run Murl's plays until the sun went behind a specific tenement building at our East River public practice field. I shudder to think how long Coach Thrush would have gone on if we had lights. He often sent his son to bring him a hot dog from a street vendor. I retain the image of Murl shivering in a cold drizzle, hot dog in one hand, those index cards in the other, and a cigarette on his lower lip.

Another image that needs no recollection is our team portrait in spring 1962 on the stage at Stuyvesant HS for our yearbook picture (Fig. page 26). We were all in our jackets and ties (and most of us with white socks peering out from under dark pants), and the only representative of the coaching staff was Coach Murl.

In college, we did not scrimmage every day, but at Stuyvesant we did, except maybe the Friday before a Saturday game. After a long practice, Murl then made his way to his New Jersey home, and we to ours in the boroughs, on buses and the subway, our gear slung over our shoulders. Of course, we were always thrilled and energized by Coach Thrush's final admonition on game eve: "And don't forget your jockey strap!"

Murl somehow forged us seniors into a team. We engaged in a three-way preseason scrimmage with Erasmus and Midwood at the latter's Brooklyn field. And we more than held our own. I felt us melding into a unit, and we loved each other, truly. Still, not much was expected of us seniors, but then early in the fall we got the best of a Xavier team in a scrimmage on our shared practice field. Murl said their coaches "were sick" about their charges' performance. Later, in fall practice when I was handling a lineman over me (I was an offensive guard), Murl said I had "blood in my eye." We all appreciated that coach was one tough cookie, and compliments like that went a long way.

Murl was a master psychologist, as are all successful coaches. For instance, he played to our ethnic backgrounds. We had a little room off the raised circular track in our building, hemmed in on all sides with tenements or mean streets, not a green blade of grass in our real estate footprint. In that little room where we worked out and were assessed for quickness and coordination, Coach Thrush asked if I were Italian American. He made me feel good about being a part of the lineage of good Italian players from Stuyvesant.

On an earlier occasion he asked me what I was—the intent to find me a position. I understood that, and since I didn't know I just said, "Nothing."

For Murl, that was a teachable moment. "Nothing? You're a nothing?" To the others: "This guy sez he's a nothing." It sounded so damning in his "salivary drawl" as he went on. Oh man, did he piss me off, and if that was his intent, he succeeded.

This was part of the impetus for accelerated development. We felt that the other teams were ahead of us in age, physical maturity, and training, so we worked hard. During the cold weather of the early spring semester, we had Saturday "tryouts in Central Park," run by the upcoming seniors. I'm sure it was against the regulations of the Public School Athletic League. Thrush was never there—drill sergeant seniors put us through our paces. I barely recovered by Sunday night.

And then, in time, I became a Central Park Arctic drill sergeant.

The Stuyvesant gym was too small for home basketball games, but it was large enough for pad-less scrimmages, frustrating because John Hagopian (one of the quickest guys I ever faced) always had his shoulder in my face before I could get out of my stance, and I was known for being quick off the ball in college.

Football was not just about wins and losses. Personnel, both on the team and peripheral to it, were integral to the experience, and to my education:

Ms. Perrucci. She was 40-ish, a spry, petite, and attractive teacher of Spanish and history. I believe she took students of Italian descent under her wing, though she never articulated that to me. We got along famously, until she learned that I had turned down an invitation to participate in an advanced math class. Now, understand, this was Stuyvesant, where guys went very far with purely mathematical projects in the Westinghouse National Science Scholar competition; where kids placed high in the International Math Olympiad, and like that.

How could I keep my head above water in that class? The question was ringing in my head.

I turned down the invitation. It was fall football season, so there was a conflict, at least that was my cop-out. Ms. Perrucci called me on the carpet.

"What are you doing? This is a great opportunity!"

"I can't attend the class. It interferes with football practice."

She was livid with exasperation. "Football? Are you going to play professionally?"

I don't think I answered verbally. But even then, I knew that football was not a career option. Ms. Perrucci read the negative answer in my demeanor.

I don't recall how the conversation ended, only that I crawled away from it.

Funny, I was insecure about my intellectual abilities, but lack of experience and size did not keep me away from high school football. Well, maybe not so funny.

Julius Rothenberg. He was a popular English teacher, known to play his violin to accompany sob stories about lost homework, or tossing an unabridged dictionary with a blind hook shot at students guilty of a malaprop. He was a well-groomed clown in his tweed jacket and tie, but his love of English was genuine.

I never knew the dynamic between Messrs. Thrush and Rothenberg, but it's hard to imagine teachers of such disparate disciplines and backgrounds. Mr. R probably had an impressive résumé, full of articles in prestigious literary journals. But I came to appreciate his contributions to *MAD Magazine*. The following *MAD* filler is one, and I resurrect it purely from memory:

Bali Hi Edges Newman Eleven 70–7. The score may have been more lopsided. The story had a quote from Coach "Thurl Mush" and described the Newman Eleven's only score by dint of a "Bali player running back an interception the wrong way." Oh yes, old-timers will recognize Alfred E Newman, the life force of *MAD*, kind of a humanized Howdy Doody from Geppetto's workshop. A smiling AE Newman in one of those leather football helmets was a natural for MAD.

I feel obliged to offer this explanation to my otherwise very well-educated fiftysomething daughter: "Laura, Bali Hi (or Hai) is a Rogers and Hammerstein song to an island, from the Broadway musical 'South Pacific.' Ezio Pinza sang a memorable duet of it with Mary Martin."

Long Snaps. We were practicing coverage on punts. Our center was not doing a great job getting the ball back to Coach Thrush standing in the punter's position. The ball sailed over Coach's head, or reached him on a bounce, or sailed wide, left and right. Murl was frustrated. Finally, he yelled to our center, "(. . .) hit me in the pecker!"

Despite his poor marksmanship, our center was a hero to me for overcoming a disability to play football. He was also a very funny guy. He invited me to attend a dance at his Lower East Side Jewish center. Entering, I was confronted by large Hebrew letters over a stage that featured a steel drum band. The crowd of mostly Latino and Black kids was dancing and having a blast. The place was throbbing, far from ecclesiastical (contemplative). My buddy was there, welcoming me, introducing me to folks, and we joined the fun. 'Twas a memorable evening.

Mean Streets (and River). Leaving practice meant walking a few blocks to a bus or subway stop. The neighborhood field, on the East River across from Brooklyn's old Domino Sugar factory, was between the Con Ed powerplant (East 15th Street) and the Williamsburg Bridge (Delancey Street). Our field is now part of the John V. Lindsay East River Park—oh, how gentrified.

Gentrification is not the "final answer," however. Mother Nature rules. A $1.58 billion project will raise the fields by eight feet in anticipation of the next "Superstorm Sandy." According to cuz Rosalie Mangano, "we [New Yorkers] don't solve problems, we throw money at them." Maybe future Stuyvesant grads will dig more at the roots of the problem instead of uprooting trees that got in the way of *The East Side Coastal Resiliency Project*.

At least the air is cleaner today to go along with a safer neighborhood. Back then, the Lower East Side neighborhood was doubly unhealthy—atrocious air quality and dangerous residents. After practice, we tended to be hassled as we wended our way to public transportation. There was one particularly serious confrontation with one of our players who came from Little Italy. He wasn't going to take any guff, recruiting a posse that included me. But the bad guys, supposedly packing heat, did not show up. I literally dodged a bullet.

After Stuyvesant, in the pre-college summer of 1962, my high school football days were not over. I headed west to Las Vegas for a summer job. Late that summer, I was able to work out with the Bishop Gorman High School football team. It was hot and dry, yes, but I was never as stressed as I was back on the summer shores of the East River.

The aunts and uncles of my Bensonhurst youth, at the short-lived bar in our store basement/storage area (1966).

Left to Right: Aunt Millie, Uncle Jijjie (on a visit from Las Vegas), Uncle Gregory, and Mamma. Gregory was stepdad's brother and Millie his wife. Their kids were my cousins, and I was very close to his family.

Jijjie from glitzy Vegas never cast aspersion on that cave-like bar.

Chapter Five

. . .

UNCLE JIJJIE
(1962)

> My Unc Jijjie, he no Vegas fool
> He know the score without goin' to school
> From Brooklyn expat to desert rat
> Uncle Jijjie be where they at.
> Y'all sho' can take on that,
> As one un-honed honest fact

My family is small, especially for an immigrant Italian family—my mother and her three siblings were first generation, born in America to immigrant parents from Naples. My biological father, also first generation but from Bari, was out of our life by the time I was five and contact with his side went silent for about sixty years.

Men escaping the hearth extended to my maternal Neapolitan grandfather. He flew the coop, deserting my grandmother, my Nonna, who never fully mastered English due to a hearing

Uncle Ben in the WWII Navy (1942). Compare his visage with the "choir boy" figure on page 14. He was MIA for a while in the Pacific Theater.

Ben and Jijjie were loving people, though short sticks of dynamite with short fuses.

My AUNT ANGIE, Vina's kid sister, tragically passed at 26 in a one-car accident in Vegas. Her son Ben became Little Ben, and was adopted by his Uncle Ben, who became his father.

impairment. Meningitis in the old country was blamed for Nonna's hearing deficiency, just as Guido Trapani's parents lost all their hearing to childhood meningitis (*The Mouthpiece [1940]*). I think genetics, and not meningitis, was responsible for hearing loss in several members of my immediate family. Whatever her affliction, my very hard-of-hearing, single-parent grandma, my Nonna, nurtured a family of five through the Depression, and beyond.

In La Puma's Bensonhurst, and mine, we used the ugly term "deaf and dumb." But Nonna was not 'Dumb'—she could speak Neapolitan dialect **loudly**, along with a few unrepeatable choice English words. My mamma, Vina, was the third of four children, and Nonna's first girl (page 14). She was a surrogate mom to her siblings and her hearing held out during those years.

But males did come to the fore. Vina's brothers, my Uncles Ben and Johnny (Jijjie), became major breadwinners. Jijjie claimed he once was the youngest master carpenter in New York at nineteen, circa 1940. The brothers were tender-hearted, but tough. Jijjie had the creds: Golden Gloves boxing champ and undefeated in several professional bouts. And Ben was no slouch—both had scary tempers.

Japan attacked Pearl Harbor (and other US Pacific bases) on December 7, 1941. Soon after, Jijjie and Ben enlisted, as did most of Sal La Puma's Bensonhurst boys. They were all loyal American citizens despite Italy being part of the Japanese-German axis. I know that before Pearl Harbor *Il Duce*, Mussolini, recruited Italian youth in Bensonhurst. My uncles saw action in the Pacific with the navy. Ben was MIA for a while. My Nonna never talked about it. Jijjie was a Seabee and specialized in underwater construction and demolition. The Seabee symbol fit Jijjie to a T: a mad bee firing a machine gun while holding a monkey wrench and a hammer.

Jijjie and Ben were lucky to be born in Little Italy and not "Big" Italy. Ezio Pinza, star of the Metropolitan Opera, Broadway, and Hollywood, was born in Big Italy and so was involuntarily "quartered" in Ellis Island under Roosevelt's Executive Order 9066, restricting movement and freedom of "domestic enemies" of the US. It must be said that Japanese Americans endured much more under the same executive order. From 1942 to 1945, people of Japanese descent, *including U.S. citizens*, were incarcerated in isolated detention camps.

After the war, Ben settled in the L.A. area and worked as a master carpenter. Uncle Jijjie flew off to the Las Vegas boom town where he had connections in the construction industry. He took part in the construction of the Sands Hotel. I spent the summer of '62, between Stuyvesant High School and Cornell University, in that wide-open town where I met some wild and colorful characters.

To me, Jijjie Grandi was one of the most colorful and toughest. He was not tall, but wiry, his "re-chiseled" nose testimony to combat. His eyes were boiling tar pits, and they gave short warning when he was about to erupt, which he did frequently. But that summer, I felt absolutely loved. Unc seemed to dig that I was going the conventional route of entering college that fall. And Uncle Ben was completely on board with it, as well. I was fulfilling a dream that had been out of reach for them (though both hurdled early barriers to continue their educations).

In Vegas, Uncle Jijjie did not discourage my own nerdy interests and tendencies, such as collecting weird desert insects and reptiles. The image I projected to others was burnished by playing in a local baseball league and working out in late summer with the Bishop Gorman football team. Also, I had a manual labor job at the downtown Fremont Hotel and Casino (and, thanks to

Head of Engineering Jijjie Grandi, it was *inside*, out of the daytime heat).

Athletics and hard work made me acceptable to the locals, though Uncle Jijjie's love was unconditional (*if* I made my bed daily and kept the bathroom vanity clean). In addition to neatness, Uncle Jijjie valued hard work, drive, and sincerity in others, no matter their occupation or social level. He was at home with a range of characters, from casino executives to dealers to bouncers. (Vegas was an intersection of many worlds. Some of the latino umps in my baseball league worked at the Fremont—they were refugees from Cuban casinos shut down by Castro.)

For our summer weekday routine, Uncle Jijjie and I got to work early, shared a breakfast in a casino restaurant/coffee shop, and then headed off to our jobs. On our arrival one morning, the attendant at the Fremont Hotel parking garage looked more than a little concerned:

"Mr. Grandi, there's a man walking around here with no pants."

"Don't worry, honey, I'll check it out."

So, we cruised the lanes and came across a guy who was a dead ringer for Ernie Kovacs, black curly hairdo, thick mustache, suit, and tie, but boxer shorts *sans* pants exposing good shoes and dress socks. Jijjie got out of the car and confronted the guy, who towered over my uncle.

"Hey, buddy, what are you doin' here?"

He was drunk out of his mind, looking down into the eyes of my unc, who had his chin stuck in the guy's chest. Kovacs said something incomprehensible.

"Get your ass out of here before somebody gets hurt," growled Uncle Jijjie.

Security was not called, and the pantless Kovacs lookalike retreated, virtually disappearing. Suddenly, the crisis was over.

I was so impressed that security was not called—there was no violence, no guns. (Uncle Jijjie certainly wasn't carrying heat.) We simply went on to our respective workdays, nothing out of the usual in this desert fantasy kingdom. Uncle Jijjie had no idea if the guy was a serial killer, or if he was armed.

Does anyone recall Brooklynite Eddie Murphy's shtick? *"Nobody mess with you if they think you crazy."* I keep thinking of that armed, aggressive, mad Seabee.

Death is only a life stage. The similarity between Kovacs and the pantless interloper was so strong I thought the guy might have been the real Ernie Kovacs, in Vegas for a show. Then I recalled that Kovacs had tragically passed in a one-car accident a few months before, in January 1962 while I was still in high school. (Most readers may not know of Kovacs, an iconoclastic TV character/pioneer in the early days of the medium.)

I bet that Mamma Vina would have been susceptible to the suggestion that Kovacs's widow, Edie Adams, channeled Ernie's spirit for a partial—*sans* pants—return to Vegas. Spiritism and the evil eye (*malocchio*) were common beliefs among the immigrant classes, and they were rife in Bensonhurst, mine and La Puma's. The characters in Salvatore's stories communicated with the dead—with a deceased father appearing in a basement mirror (*The Gangster's Ghost [1939]*) or with grandfather in his casket, his spirit roused by his grandson to go crabbing in Gravesend Bay (*Wear It in Good Health [1943]*). Death was not so much an ending as a prelude to further adventure. Even grandfather's dog, Garibaldi, understood this—Garibaldi and García-Márquez.

Mothers and the evil eye (*'o malocchio*). Vina never wanted to brag about her first grandchild, Laura (born 1970 in the early developing stages of my "manhood"). Mamma was afraid of attracting the evil eye (the *maloik* in street lingo) from jealous grandmothers. They were not necessarily evil, just that their envy could inadvertently trip an evil spirit attack. A nice old neighborhood Neapolitan, *nu vicchiariello 'e vicenato*, advised us to go to Little Italy to pick up the "horn," or *cornetto*, to ward off the *maloik*. The cornetto looks like a golden chili pepper, a pendant commonly worn by the *goombahs* (Italian "friends" in street dialect) of Bensonhurst. If one is caught unarmed, without such hardware, the eye could be warded off by a manual martial art: the thumb holding the middle two fingers down, while horn points formed by the pinkie and pointer fingers are directed at evil. The old ladies in black used this gesture against Carmine, the cad who ignored the love of Julia, driving her to attempt suicide (*Gravesend Bay [1940]*).

Dear reader, a spoiler alert: Skip the next five lines, and go to Chapter Six.

Julia's suicide attempt brought mixed results. She lived, but lost the cad, Carmine Carmellini. Triple-C, however, became a good guy, a fireman who married Jewish Patricia. He also became a great runner and a wonderful father. (He always could sing.)

The "digital cornetto" was at least partially responsible.

Seated: Polacco, Zimmerman, Mr. Cavallaro, Grauna, Hott, Freundlich.
2nd Row: Ross, Pearl, Savedoff, Zwerin, Friedman, Greiff, Dix.
3rd Row: Morris, Belsky, Sachs, Mariotti, Diaz.

Stuyvesant High School Baseball, 1962. In college, I was to learn that boxing was no way to make a living. However, it took me longer to give up the dream of a baseball career. In my senior year, I went out for the Stuyvesant team, and made it as a utility outfielder and backup catcher (to excellent Pete Grauna). We had enough talent to win the Manhattan championship, but our city dreams were dashed by Staten Island's Curtis High. Among their stars was Terry Crowley who had a long career as player and coach with the Orioles and Reds. In three world series, Crowley batted 0.286 with some big hits.

Note several names on both the baseball and football rosters. We tended to recycle athletic talent.

Chapter Six

• • •

NO WAY TO MAKE A LIVING
(1962, 1966)

Keep your youthful verve and innocence
Away from old men's grasping avarice
They crave your passion's omnipotence
Draining it to feed a hunger cadaverous

I was a high school senior when boxer Emile Griffith III killed Benny "Kid" Paret in the ring at Madison Square Garden, three subway stops uptown from Stuyvesant HS. The setting was a welterweight championship fight. Technically, Paret did not die in the ring. He went into a coma at the end of the fight and died ten days later, March 31, 1962. Emile, born in St. Thomas, Virgin Islands, was not a stereotypical boxer. He designed ladies' hats. He was a great dancer in and out of the ring and, in the jargon of the time, "he walked both sides of the street." In the weigh-in for the heralded fight, the rubber match of three, Champion Paret, a Cuban, called Griffith a *maricón*, roughly "gay," but decidedly more derogatory. Most agree, if only in retrospect, that in the 12th and last scheduled round the referee should have been more aggressive in coming between Paret and the raging Griffith. The ref claimed, also, that he did not hear Paret's handlers yelling to stop the fight.

Now, understand, today I have trouble stomaching a prize fight, but back then the fights very much appealed to me and to the public at large. The fight game was also a ladder up for immigrants. My heroes included Brooklynites Paddy DeMarco, Joey Giardello, Rocky Graziano, and other Italian American champs such as Rocky Marciano and Carmen Basilio. Note, these guys were not just American champs, but World Champs, especially when weight divisions were not divided into an alphabet soup of WBA, IBF, WBO, and WBC councils, federations, et *al.* Sure, many bouts were fixed, and many fighters shamelessly exploited, but the lure of a championship fight was irresistible to me and to the public at large. A boxer was a local celebrity, as was La Puma's Rocco, "killer in the ring and with dames" (*The Boys of Bensonhurst [1942]*).

No matter the Paret tragedy, Griffith had to defend his regained title. He did so, July 23, 1962, in the Las Vegas Convention Center against Ralph Dupas, and I was there. I did not swing a ticket. Uncle Jijjie graciously gave me his. He could swing my job, but he apparently couldn't come up with a third ticket at the last minute. I witnessed the Dupas-Griffith match accompanied by Uncle Jijjie's new wife, Jean. The crowd in the convention center was electric, and with undercurrents: It was a championship match and Griffith's first match after his tragic encounter with Paret, just four months before. The air was heavy with smoke, and interactions among the crowd told me there was more going on than just a fight—and not just because gambling was legal. I could read knowing looks, as if I were Aunt Jean's boytoy. But I could not shake the larger impression that the sheer humanity and interest in the match dwarfed the boxers. They did not drive the event, but were transformed by external motive forces into pugilistic mannequins.

Griffith had a double victory that night. He outpointed a game and talented Ralph Dupas, and he kept his devil at bay, especially in the twelfth and last round when he had Dupas on the ropes. Dupas lived to fight another day. He defeated Denny Moyer the next year, 1963, for the light welterweight crown.

Dupas was from a large and poor family in New Orleans's French Quarter. Throughout his career, he fought top contenders and champs, including the legendary Sugar Ray Robinson to whom he lost on an unpopular split decision. Dupas started boxing at the age of fourteen, by lying on his application that he was the legal minimum age of eighteen. He had well over one hundred professional fights, and they took a toll.

That toll was obvious to me four years later, in late summer, 1966. I was again in Vegas, after an arduous hike up from Central America (Chapter Thirteen). I had graduated college in June '66, followed by an eight-week summer stint in Central America—my last undergraduate "activity." Uncle Jijjie invited me to attend a few bouts in his boxing club on top of the Fremont Hotel. A small but capacity crowd filled the limited space and applauded appreciatively when Vegas resident and former heavyweight champ Sonny Liston was introduced before the night's festivities. Sonny graciously stood and waved to the assembled.

The main event paired Ralph Dupas with a Las Vegas sanitation worker. I sat ringside as did virtually all in attendance in the intimate space. It was easy to see that Dupas was laboring and hurting. He was decisively beaten—the fight was stopped in the eighth round.

The next morning, I was sitting next to my uncle at a table in a Fremont office. Others in attendance were a sports columnist for the Vegas morning paper, Dupas's manager, and at least one other guy—I think the state boxing commissioner. I had read that day's column by the journalist in which he made a strong appeal to "retire" Dupas, who was clearly damaged goods. Dupas's manager listened stoically, and then declared that they had four months to prepare for the next bout. End of discussion, seemingly.

Dupas lived another forty-two years to age seventy-two (1935–2008). He was so brain damaged over the last several years of his life that he couldn't get out of bed to attend his 2000 induction into the Boxing Hall of Fame. I am also told that his last match was a knockout loss, in the eighth round, to Joe Clark of Las Vegas, in 1966. Perhaps then, Ralph's manager did not prevail, and Dupas was put out to pasture after that fight. So, I saw two of Ralph's last fights, both losses, one "honorable" and one just plain tragic.

Speaking of honor and tragedy, Emile Griffith made peace with the son of Benny Paret, an encounter featured in *Ring of Fire*, a 2005 documentary (directors Ron Berger and Dan Klores). Five years after Dupas's death, Emile passed, in 2013. A small part of his legacy is the beautiful quote: "I kill a man and most forgive me. . . . I love a man, and many say this makes me an evil person." (*A Man's World: The Double Life of Emile Griffith*. Donald McRae, Simon and Schuster, 2015).

No matter the big wins, boxers always lose the last bout. Four years after Las Vegas's Joe Clark TKO'd Ralph Dupas, Sonny Liston was found dead in his Vegas home, apparently of an overdose. But talk on the street persisted that Sonny was the victim of a mob hit in retaliation for not taking a dive. Liston was 38. He was reportedly averse to drugs.

Liston's house did not move well on the Vegas real estate market. Uncle Jijjie bought the house at a good price. Mary and I, with our two-year-old Laura, were hosted in the house before moving to our first real jobs, in early 1972.

I boxed a little in college—I had a predilection for taking head blows, not just in boxing, but also in rugby, football, and catching foul balls on my catcher's mask. However, one of the greatest university lessons to penetrate my thick, Southern Italian skull, my *capo dosto*, was that boxing was no way to make a living.

  But it's really about the Bensonhurst I knew growing up in the '60s and '70s. The Bensonhurst where the little old Italian ladies went out with their cart and shopped at seven stores along Bath Ave.

—Steve Schirripa

Chapter Seven

• • •

SCHOOL OF HARD KNOCKS
(1962, 1963)

> A head full of resentment
> And of righteous discontent
> Can make you a Battering Ram
> Against those that you damn

As they said in Bensonhurst, sometimes you need a hard head, a *capo dosto*, whether or not you get physically knocked.

In my freshman year at Cornell, my botany professor was Dr. Harlan Parker Banks, a paleobotanist of renown. He studied very old plants, though he was vivacious in his middle age so that his lectures were fun. He was creative in his teaching, such as providing the class with diced morsels of watermelon to stress the crunchy nature of the plant cell wall. Graduate students ran the teaching labs, and Dr. Banks gave all the lectures. His exams were challenging, but fair. In the middle of the course's second semester (Botany II), I took an hour-long "prelim" exam, which was essentially the basis of my midsemester grade. There was a tricky genetics question for which I gave the "obvious" answer, until I realized that I had made a wrong assumption (about maternal versus filial gene expression). At the call for handing in papers, I crossed out my answer and scribbled the correct one, which I circled and indicated with a large arrow. I received zero credit for the question, which only a handful in a class of over one hundred had answered correctly.

What to do? This was well before the days of email, texting, and course websites, now common ways of communicating with an instructor. Professor Banks did not announce office hours. I could just let the situation pass but getting full credit would have put me on my way to an A. Putting grade considerations aside, I was unfairly "shafted." I needed to speak up, so I steeled my resolve. Stomach churning, I approached Dr. Banks after the next lecture. I explained my late realization of how to answer the question, and that I had indeed put down the correct answer, which I showed him. He took my exam and talked in generalities about "memory banks" and how this would be considered in future performance evaluations. I received no further communication from Dr. Memory Banks.

My midsemester grade, based on that exam, was the numerical equivalent of a D. I did not approach Dr. Banks again. Apparently, after our talk he had gone over all my exam answers very critically, and he found fault in some of them. We had been warned about this situation—as a batter don't question the umpire's call or for the rest of the game you'll have an expanded strike zone. It was apparent also that I received zero credit for the genetics question in dispute. I say "apparent" because the exam was never returned to me. It took the rest of the semester to raise my final grade to the B range.

Hey, Joe. You sound like a "grade-grubber."

Let me answer that—the situation was one of honor and justice, academic or otherwise. My mother and her brothers Ben and Jijjie often said, "Joe, you can't be a macaroni." In other words, "Don't go soft and bend when you're in hot water. Stand up for yourself." Harden that spine along with that *capo dosto.*

An Outer Banks Addendum. At the University of Missouri (MU) I resolved to be a more accessible prof. than Cornell's Dr. Banks. I was "Joe" to most MU undergraduate students working in my lab. But have we gone too far in this other direction? Student evaluations of professors have become an all-too-powerful metric of a professor's teaching performance. I know I have "taught the evaluation" rather than inflict academic anxiety on students. Like stock markets, students hate uncertainty, poor kids.

I initially came across student evaluations in my first grad student year at Duke. (Yes, I'm jumping the timeline a little, but this appears a good spot for an editorial announcement.) As a student-initiated guide to fellow students about what to expect from a professor, and pitfalls to avoid, the evaluation is a good idea. However, the system has been incorporated into the general evaluation of "teaching performance" by deans of instruction, and as such the evaluation has devolved to a measure of popularity. And part of my problem is that I always believed in challenging students eventually to lead them to the "correct" answer, the academic version of Coach Vince Lombardi's "no pain, no gain." Early at Missouri, quick quips and one-liners in my Brooklyn brogue were not appreciated. Students, especially non-science majors, tended to feel threatened, the opposite of my intention.

How would I have assessed/evaluated Dr. Banks? In Bensonhurstese, "don't ask." I think I would have taken him to task for his lack of accessibility, evidence that he did not "like" his students. (In Dr. Banks's defense, each semester of botany entertained a combined 200-plus students in two different sections, and I imagine that his other professional and academic obligations weighed on him.)

And don't get me started on grade inflation. A case can be made for the correlation of grade inflation and the growing importance of student evaluations of professors. At a faculty meeting well over twenty years ago, our department chair claimed that the average GPA of graduating seniors was B+. They would have collectively qualified for the Dean's List during my undergraduate days.

Bensonhurst vs Ithaca. Did I miss Bensonhurst while I was up there above Cayuga's waters? I confess that I did—at first. That freshman year brought two semesters each of calculus, botany/botany lab, zoology/zoology lab, chemistry/chemistry lab, and most scary of all, freshman English. Fall semester also brought football injury and the Cuban Missile Crisis. But I was not in a convent, as was Sal La Puma's beautiful nun, Cristina. She left her convent because she missed Bensonhurst (*The Jilted Groom [1940]*), and then she missed the convent. Like Cristina, I could not wait to get home to Bensonhurst. On my first Thanksgiving break, I took the subway from the Manhattan Port Authority bus terminal to the West End Bay Parkway station. I walked through our linoleum store, and upon reaching those three rooms behind it, I immediately missed Cornell.

I asked myself,

Joe, you were Bensonhurst born and raised, so how could you liken Ithaca to the neighborhood school of hard knocks?

Maybe I'm getting carried away equating mean grading in Ithaca with practices on the mean streets of the 'hood. One street practice was "business insurance." Protection money against hard knocks was common in the 'hood. The agents exacting premiums wore fedoras, as Mr. La Puma would describe them. I doubt that "protection" was a business practice in Ithaca.

La Puma's Leone, the proprietor of a pastry shop in Little Italy, wasn't verbally "convincing" against insistent fedoras. He was obliged to blast two *vile traviatóre*, vile rats, with his long-barreled shotgun when he was pushed to set up a protection contract. When Leone moved his *pasticceria* from Little Italy to Bensonhurst, he was left alone (*Guys Under Their Fedoras [1943]*).

Stepdad told me he kicked some "gorillas" out of our store when they pushed him to buy protection. (He used the Neapolitan *cazzoni*, as if Sicilians would not act that way.) Over the years, I never saw Stepdad come close to backing down, in the store or on the road where angry young guys twice threatened to break his nose—road rage before it had a name. Stepdad's *schnoz* was already especially aquiline from "nasal accidents"—a genetic trait environmentally enhanced. When offered yet another free "nose job," he just responded,

"Oh, yeah? Let's see you try."

Both times he was in the driver's seat, window down, his nose a tempting target. One guy was a motorcycle honcho, with his gang in tow, and the other a *pazzo* (crazy man) in a car trying to pass us on one-way single lane 85th Street as Stepdad looked for an address to collect on a bill. My presence in the passenger seat was not much of a deterrent. On both occasions, the guys just walked away cursing. For a guy so worried about his health, Stepdad had little regard for bodily injury in a fight.

Now, fifty-seven years after my Cornell graduation, I ask if Bensonhurst and Ithaca were so diametrically opposite. Did Yale make New Haven a Shangri-la? Did Harvard do the same for Cambridge? (I conjure toga-clad mob figures at sit-downs.) There really are no discrete quanta of differences; some of us try to inhabit the "good" side of an amorphous ethical gradient.

Hard Knocks on the Gridiron. While pondering nuclear annihilation during the fall '62 Cuban Missile Crisis, I experienced personal annihilation on the football field. I went out for the Cornell freshman football team, encouraged by Stuyvesant HS teammate Randy Zimmerman. (NCAA regulations back then prohibited freshmen from playing on the varsity.) As an offensive guard, maxing out at a very bulked-up 180 pounds, I was still way too light, especially given the "sumo wrestling" style of blocking by >200-pound linemen. Pulling guards (like me) were not so much in vogue as they were in high school. But things started looking up. I was getting more playing time at linebacker, and I managed to move up the depth charts, aided by injuries to teammates ahead of me. Then it was my turn. My knee got whacked in a scrimmage and there went most of my freshman season, though I did come back at season's end.

Freshman football had its positives, mostly off the field. Teammates couldn't believe I played the O-line, and the juxtaposition of NYC and high school football was to some incongruous, if I may use a couple of Ivy League words. The center of the football universe seemed to be eastern Ohio/western Pennsylvania, since most players came from there. Their cross-border banter was hilarious. Oh, yes, the team included a few prep school graduates, and I believe one was Peter Pinza, son of the late opera star Ezio. I had enough interaction with Pete to know not to call him a preppie. He was a regular guy and a tough running back.

Another positive was colorful coaches. Frosh coach Ted Thoren was behind his desk at Teagle Hall when I picked up my gear at the beginning of fall practice. He looked up as I walked by his office to the locker room.

"Hey! Where you goin' with that?"

My head was hidden by the shoulder pads, helmet, and practice gear I was embracing. I imagine I looked like an overloaded worker ant. He could not see my face as I responded,

"I'm going out for football."

"Oh, yeah? What position? The ball?"

At the time, I did not think it was funny, but Coach Thoren let me suit up and work out. I played more than a down or two that season. Coach loved to call me "Pole-yocko," I guess because it made me more Slavic, closer to a coal miner (a cherished trade in eastern OH/western PA).

Coach Thoren, of partial Balkan extraction, would get on players of Slavic origin. A favorite target was a large, slow-moving lineman who was usually late to respond to the whistle for scrimmage.

"[. . .], get your Slovenian ass here! If I whistled for lunch, you wouldn't be last!"

Then, in a lower voice to the assembled, "and if I yelled for [a collective feline reference to alluring young ladies] you'd be first."

The player's name just popped into my head as I write this, but there it will stay until I have a beer with fellow alums.

Coach Ted Thoren was indeed a piece of work. "Add more water to the soup, Ma, I'm coming home!" he yelled when an assignment was missed or someone was "dogging it." That spring he became varsity baseball head coach and was at it long enough to be Cornell's all-time winningest coach in any sport.

Winter Was Winter and Spring Was Sprung on Me. Weather became another hard knock. Summer held on for a while. And fall was glorious, but I was not equipped for winter, neither psychologically, biologically, nor apparel-wise. "This is Ithaca, New York, Joe," I reminded myself. Yes, I was woefully ill-prepared for the cold and the snow and the icy climb up the library slope to my eight a.m. chemistry class. I was amazed at how upstaters and New Englanders totally embraced winter.

Cornell did indeed field strong ski and hockey teams, especially the latter. The Ken Dryden hockey era started the season after my 1966 graduation. The rest of the Ivy League bemoaned the Canada-Ithaca underground railroad. Sorry, guys, Dryden was a genuine scholar-athlete. He won many non-sports honors besides being a member of the Hockey Hall of Fame. (I wonder if he chose Cornell for its more tropical climate.)

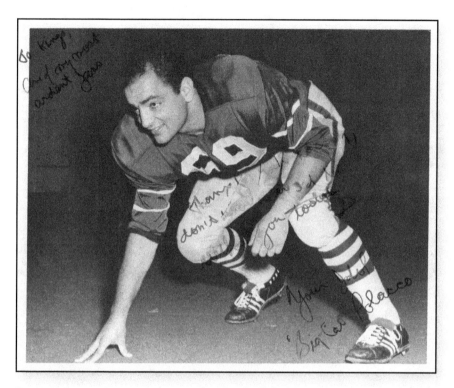

By senior year I was cocky on the football field, making All-League as a *lightweight football league* offensive lineman. I'm glad the picture is not to scale—I was required to weigh in at 154 pounds, or less, 48 hours before kick-off. The lightweight league was full of feisty little, frustrated guys from Army, Navy, Rutgers, Penn, Princeton, Columbia, and of course, Cornell.

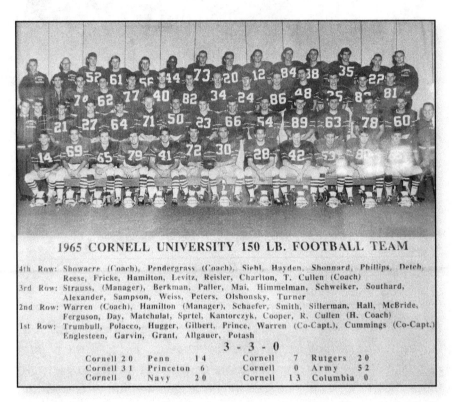

1965 CORNELL UNIVERSITY 150 LB. FOOTBALL TEAM

4th Row: Showacre (Coach), Pendergrass (Coach), Siehl, Hayden, Shonnard, Phillips, Detch, Reese, Fricke, Hamilton, Levitz, Reisler, Charlton, T. Cullen (Coach)

3rd Row: Strauss, (Manager), Berkman, Paller, Mai, Himmelman, Schweiker, Southard, Alexander, Sampson, Weiss, Peters, Olshonsky, Turner

2nd Row: Warren (Coach), Hamilton (Manager), Schaefer, Smith, Sillerman, Hall, McBride, Ferguson, Day, Matchulat, Sprtel, Kantorczyk, Cooper, R. Cullen (H. Coach)

1st Row: Trumbull, Polacco, Hugger, Gilbert, Prince, Warren (Co-Capt.), Cummings (Co-Capt.) Englesteen, Garvin, Grant, Allgauer, Potash

3 - 3 - 0

Cornell 20	Penn	14	Cornell	7	Rutgers 20
Cornell 31	Princeton	6	Cornell	0	Army 52
Cornell 0	Navy	20	Cornell	13	Columbia 0

We may have been small, but there were a lot of us. Our coach, Bob Cullen, passed in 1996. His son, Terry, took over and is still head coach. Show me a college program with that kind of mutual commitment. (I'm #69, front row.)

Chapter Eight

. . .

APRIL IS THE CRUELEST MONTH
(1963)

April is the cruellest [*sic*] month, breeding
Lilacs out of the dead land, mixing
Memory and desire, stirring
Dull roots with spring rain.
Winter kept us warm, covering
Earth in forgetful snow, feeding
A little life with dried tubers.

—TS Eliot (*The Waste Land,* 1922)

Freshman year finally brought April '63, a springtime of hope. Then, "mixing memory and desire," it played cruel tricks. As Eliot said, it was the cruelest month. Freshman English did not help my mood. First, I was expected to express an answer, and LIVE in class, *oy vey*, and there were no correct answers, double *oy vey*. In math, quadratic equations had at most two answers, and one was clearly nonsense. Second, following HL Mencken's entertaining, witty, and biting critiques of America, English had us reading dystopic poetry. We were taken on a dark turn south via morose, almost apocalyptical verse by Ezra Pound, TS Eliot, et al. In his opening verse to *The Waste Land,* Thomas Stearns Eliot presented classical signs of depression. Pardon my paraphrasing, TSE. April was Eliot's wake-up alarm, but he couldn't get out of bed—let me snooze *with dried tubers*, lie almost catatonic under my *blanket of snow.*

Cornell spring '63 was waking, stirring, and getting out of bed. I was also stirring, but Nature's awakening, its eternal forward movement, threatened to drop me behind. The gorges of Fall and Cascadilla Creeks that encircled most of campus were etched over eons, archiving millions of Aprils in their petrified stacks. And now, the baseball season of April 1963 was being written without me. I know it sounds maudlin, mourning a spring cultural blink over geological time. After all, are baseball dynasties not ephemeral? Just how immortal are those enshrined in Cooperstown? But for me, the *now* was the immediate reality: Baseball not only abandoned Brooklyn's Ebbets Field, it also was no longer part of my life. Baseball was my desire but only my memory.

The game was joyous, a true rite of spring. The rituals of practice could be more meaningful than the games themselves—running down fly balls off a fungo bat, warming up the pitcher, taking cuts in batting practice, the birdlike chatter-chirping of the infield dance of snagging hard grounders in the hole and digging them out of the dirt, pivoting at second, and throwing out phantom runners on the base paths. This celebration of spring was played on grass and real dirt. The late Dick (not Richie) Allen, who should have been in the Hall of Fame, said it best of artificial turf: "If a horse can't eat it, I don't want to play on it." But I wasn't playing on *any* surface. "Is baseball over? Is this April moving on without me?"

"No!" Fighting inertia, I went out for the freshman baseball team.

I hung on throughout tryouts until that final *cruelest cut*—I could read the look on Coach's face as he approached. Even though I was out, he gave me an out: I could work out with the varsity whose new coach was Ted Thoren, my freshman football coach. There *had* to be collusion between Thoren and the freshman baseball coach.

That spring, I learned that catching batting practice (BP) was not nearly so joyous when I was chained behind the plate. However, I networked some: One of my BP pitchers, Larry Darrah, became a University of Missouri colleague some twenty years later. I made the most of my ten-swing reward at the end of each BP, and I was alive, not Eliot's morose, fraying, balding, ageing, dying Prufrock.

If I weren't so intimidated by freshman English, I might have considered a career in poetry. Naaaaaahhh, far from it, but my tendencies were more poetic as spring erased all vestiges of snow and ice from the depths of the gorges. Back in the library, I was engaged in Professor Laubengayer's *Principles of Chemistry* when a wasp wafted in on a warm air wave through an open window: shiny purple metallic body of shimmering iridescence, so complex in all its moving parts—six jointed legs, four diaphanous wings, compound eyes, probing antennae, biting mouth parts, that awesome stinger/ovipositor, and its impossibly threadlike waist. This little creature was much more wondrous than oxidation-reduction, conservation of mass and charge, periodic groupings of the elements, chemical equilibria—it was a sensing, walking, flying wonder—a coordinated miracle.

I almost enjoyed that a gal who intimidated me in English class was close to screaming, recoiling from the wasp in horror. I would have defended the wasp if she had tried to squash it with her notebook. Indeed, I defended many small critters (spiders, beetles, caterpillars, etc.) before and since. Oh, yes, a gal, a classmate. She was not my mate, and I certainly lacked class. I was so unaccustomed to females in the classroom—and they were so different from those aggressive young ladies of lower Manhattan's Mabel Dean Bacon HS of Nursing Annex, the ladies who formed a gauntlet on my way to Stuyvesant HS from Union Square. In my Cornell freshman year, I learned much more than calculus and principles of chemistry, zoology, and botany. I learned, eventually, to be comfortable around women in the classroom. I joined a fraternity, and even had a date or two.

> While we never talked about Michelangelo
> I learned to be comfortable as milady's beau
> Into my life a gal would come and go
> I enjoyed the anticipation, and the afterglow

So, who is this TS Eliot who mourns his lost youth, who worries whether he should wear his trousers rolled? I was rejuvenated that spring of 1963, I was ready for a triumphant return to Bensonhurst, except I didn't have a summer job.

Chapter Nine

. . .

PARKIE—GREEN KID IN A CONCRETE PARK
(1963)

> Despair not a large lesson missed
> Any small experience can be said
> To offer a most nutritious grist
> For your education's daily bread

After graduating high school, a broadening summer '62 experience in Las Vegas, and a freshman year of maturation at Cornell, I found myself back in Bensonhurst for the summer of 1963, and *jobless*. What a *comedown*, as they would say in the 'hood.

But I did not mope. Stepdad's buddy, Julius Kaplan, helped me get a job with the NYC Department of Parks (NYCDP). The job was an off-campus summer educational experience, but I received no academic credits for it. Though it was in Brooklyn, it could have been "study abroad."

I was assigned to a local playground park in Brooklyn's historic Sunset neighborhood, a major site of the Revolutionary War's bloodiest battle, the August 1776 Battle of Brooklyn. In summer 1963, battles were fought in Sunset's streets, but not against the British redcoats.

Today, sixty years beyond 1963, Sunset is oh so Brooklyn hip—some of the descriptors from a Google page: *booming* Chinatown, a *diverse* Latino community, Sunset Park *with a view of the Statue of Liberty*, *pastoral* Green-Wood Cemetery, and the waterfront Industry City, *which houses creative industries and draws locals for casual artisanal eats and spirits.* (In 1963, that "City" was Bush Terminal, which, to me, was reminiscent of a huge stretch of decaying Soviet-era buildings, many of its factory lofts vacant.)

I was a summer playground assistant, "Parkie" to the neighborhood's young people. I worked with two "regulars," Cosmo, a diminutive, feisty Italian, and Irish Mike, a young upwardly mobile college graduate. Mike wore civvies, Cosmo the drab brown NYCDP uniform. His duties were more custodial, his language saltier, and his attitude super cynical. Both guys were jaded and spent as little time as possible in the park.

My job as "director of recreation" was to interact with the park's neighborhood youngsters, most of whom were Puerto Rican. One very hot day, most weren't using the wading pool, a fenced concrete enclosure with a sprinkler fountain in the middle. Several Black youngsters were in the pool, but very few Latinos.

"Why aren't you in the water?" I asked a young Latino in a bathing suit.

He shrugged, so I added, "It's hot out here, man."

He gave me a smirk, while saying, "Too many germs in the water."

Pardon this more fine-grained Italian detour on racism: It is not necessarily a Black and white concept. We Southern Italians (in general) harbored cherished negative stereotypes for immigrants from our own *Mezzogiorno*: *Calabresi* vs. *Napoletani* and *Palermitani* vs. *Sciacchitani* are only two samplers. La Puma painted all Bensonhurst Italians as Sicilian, not distinguishing those from Catania, Messina, Modica, Palermo, Sciacca, Siracusa, etc. Sal prepared us for Jewish-Sicilian marriages, but the prejudices in Bensonhurst were more textured even in my post–La Puma youth. Pairings such as *Napoletano-Palermitano* could approach the scandalous. Their families in the old country barely spoke the same language. My Neapolitan mamma learned to communicate in either, becoming a lady of greater respect in the eyes of La Puma's generic Sicilians.[3]

Back to Sunset: My park was far from pastoral. It was a concrete clearing in a forest of walk-ups and many poorly maintained four-family duplexes. The playground featured a softball diamond painted on concrete, basketball backboards, that wading pool, and swings next to reinforced concrete walls for handball. More than once, I asked people who were shooting up behind those walls to take their business elsewhere. Life is much more precious to me now, and I shiver thinking of the chances I took. Perhaps the users appreciated that I did not call the men in blue.

---

[3] I gifted Stepfather an English-Sicilian dictionary (Joseph Bellestri, MD, 1988, Ann Arbor, MI). Stepdad disagreed with many of the entries. Well, of course: Dr. Bellestri was educated in the Sicilian regions of Syracuse and Catania. Stepdad's roots were in Belmonte Mezzagno near Palermo. I'm on my cultural soapbox: There is perhaps not full appreciation of Sicilian language, and culture in general. In 1959, poet Salvatore Quasimodo (don't snicker) of Modica won the Nobel Prize in Literature. He was not the only one from the three-cornered island so honored.

On another occasion, I noted that the popular "Nok Hockey" board was missing. An informant told me the building and the landing of the board's new location. I entered the four-story walk-up. As I climbed upstairs the crescendo of puck "nok" on wooden sideboards homed me to the culprits' third-floor apartment. I knocked on the door, and the internal knocking stopped. A twenty-something guy in a sleeveless T-shirt opened the door.

"Our Nok Hockey board is here. It belongs in the park."

He gave me a resigned look, went inside, and came out with the board, hockey sticks and puck. I returned to the park, looking over my shoulder the whole way.

I was a green kid in a concrete park, but it did have some weird wildlife—both the denizens and migrants who used it as a shortcut. One guy came through daily with folded shirts and three to five pairs of work pants. I bought a couple of pairs of pants once, and Mamma was pleased—good price, and they were clean and pressed. It was obvious, even to me, that the haberdashery from his workplace was not "irregulars." (Cosmo hated the guy, especially since he bragged more than once of his sexual prowess, and how he just knew he impregnated his girlfriend on one notable love-making occasion.)

A few residents were "leftovers" from the 'hood of old, before it turned from Scandinavian-Irish to Latino. An Irish gal, too hard-edged for me to call her a colleen, was a Latina convert. Her mother was dead set against her new outlook. Daughter had a Puerto Rican boyfriend and she would broach no bad-mouthing her new culture and people. She was not one to mess with.

A lovely Swedish gal, early twenties, strolled in the park frequently. So fair-skinned and blonde, she was almost Santa Albina in that neighborhood. One day I invited her to the movies, and she accepted. On date day, the young guys were so obnoxious

I gave them a talking to, in a mix of Spanish and English. Instead of back-talking me, they looked a little contrite, to the extent that I felt bad.

An elderly Italian guy came to the park almost daily, to eat his beautiful sandwich on his favorite bench. He was frustrated that I couldn't understand his dialect. He was ancient, leathery, as wrinkled as an elephant, with the dirt of decades under his fingernails. His ears were elephantine. At times he drooled, but he was coherent. More than once he told me about life in the old country: "I work-a in the fields all day, and f——a all night."

I was still a babe in the woods, far from a man of the world. A much more worldly non-Latino guy befriended me. He often stopped to chat while on his daily way through the park. A couple of times he invited me to have a beer and a sandwich at a bar on the Bush Terminal waterfront. The bar was rundown and had some rough-looking characters, but none more threatening to me than the bartender. She was a thirty-fiveish redhead, slim, in "pedal pushers," and she tied her button-down blouse to expose a tight midriff and cleavage. Her appearance would have been entirely pleasant except for her X-rated body language: pelvic gyrations and thrusts even when mixing drinks or pouring a beer. Once, when leaning back, elbows against the back of the bar, her eyes met mine, and she asked if I were going "to rush home to. . ." Her hand pantomimed self-abuse.

My companion took it all in stride; the floor show was free. It also made me realize how green I was. On one occasion, he got serious and told me, "Next time you pick up the tab." I took his comment to mean that I should grow up, and not always be "on the take," like a kid.

Only now, in my dotage, I think he might have wanted me to tip the lady, and maybe take it from there. I was a green kid with little green in my pocket. I had no real cash that summer or any other during college. All my paychecks were endorsed over to Stepdad, who disbursed food and spending money to Mamma. While she passed a little cash on to me, I believe most came from her garment sweatshop job. (Stepdad's brother, my Uncle Gregory, shared his tips with me when I assisted him on a flooring installation. He was an angel who worked like the devil. The store was named after him—*Greg's Floor Covering*—so esteemed was he in the 'hood.)

My summer interactions, of course, were mainly with the youngsters in the park, and they presented special challenges of their own. They knew how to make my life miserable, at times tormenting me to homicidal rage.

I recall one adolescent teasingly refusing to hand over a Nok Hockey stick, and a buddy yelling, "*¡Tíralo al suelo!*"

"Oh, throw it on the ground? Is that what your parents taught you?" I yelled indignantly. They looked more surprised at my Spanish than repentant for their actions.

But I did have my favorites among the younger set. One was a charming Jamaican, maybe nine or ten. He lived in a well-maintained "attached three-story" (basement and two upper floors on each side). His place was across the street directly behind my bunker, and he dropped by often. But he could at times be a testicle twister. After all, I was one of the park's recreational attractions. One day, he was into throwing cups of water in my direction, inside the brick bunker. Lying in wait, I chased him out and caught the sonuvagun. This apprehension was witnessed by the boy's dad, a dark muscular specimen in a Caribbean-style fedora-bop hat, who came charging from across the street.

"Hey, what are you doing to my boy?"

"Oh, is this your boy? You know what he was doing?" My anger trumped my fear.

When I explained the situation, he took his boy home for some discipline. Dad and I were all right after that.

So, the job was far from boring—well, maybe boredom punctuated by intervals of frustration, rage, fear, and sometimes despair. Behind my "headquarters" within that compact brick pill box were the public bathrooms. Kids would sniff airplane glue in the stalls, and I was obliged to kick them out. They seemed to be as strung out as the older guys shooting up behind the handball court. This experience was both frustrating and despairing because the boys already seemed beyond help.

I was greeted one morning by bullet holes in the thick, opaque, wire mesh–reinforced windows of the bunker.

"What happened here?" I said to no one in particular.

"We were testing our zip guns, Parkie," said one of the park regulars.

"What the hell for?" I retorted. (Payment for damage repair was beyond the pale, not even an issue. This was on the NYCDP.)

They explained that they were having a war with Italians from a nearby neighborhood and needed heavier weaponry than the jagged-toothed slats they somehow ripped off the park benches. A .22 bullet fits snugly in the bore of the appropriate "telescoping" antenna segment from older model cars. The reader can probably figure out the rest of zip gun engineering.[4] Would that the kids were so creative and industrious in school.

---

[4] The antenna segment is the barrel, firmly mounted on a block of wood, and the .22 fired by a triggering spring device, as simple as a bent nail driven by a strong rubber band under tension. Even a cap gun can be made into a zip gun.

The gang theme was strong, and they all loved the film version of *West Side Story* (Jerome Robbins and Robert Wise, directors, 1961). What they loved the most was when the PR Sharks put it to the Jets.

"Hey, c'mon, the message of the movie is that war is no good. People die, and nothing is settled."

As Mamma would say, they looked at me with deaf eyes.

The summer wore on, the days got shorter, and I tried to be on the subway well before the end of my shift at nine, when the 'hood lived up to its Sunset name. So, I cut corners off my workday. Even walking the three or so blocks in the dusk to the subway stop seemed dangerous. I recall a very cute PR young lady who usually greeted me as I rushed by her stoop—a tempting siren on my Odyssean journey back to Bensonhurst's Greg's Floor Covering. There, another lady was happy to see me home earlier—not Homer's Penelope, but Joe's Mamma Vina.

My shortened workday brought consequences. One morning, a "gringo" type in a suit came by and gave me his card. He worked with the City of New York.

"Are you here all day?"

"Yeah, I have to be."

"When do you leave?"

"Around nine, after I lock down the equipment." (I don't recall if we closed the bathrooms.)

"Do you know Juan Montez?" (The name is fictional for this story.)

"No."

"His mother claims he was in the park before nine, and he fell and broke his arm. There was no one here to tend to him, or to call medical service."

"Sorry to hear that. Are you sure his accident was before nine?"

"That is what the affidavit says."

Ahh, just what I need, I risk my life all summer and then get fined, sued, or maybe even serve time because I saved my butt fleeing the park early.

Mr. Fancy Suit left, and I asked around. I didn't know Juan. The story I got was that he was sniffing glue. He was high on the fumes and high on the fence, and then fell, with no park personnel to come to his aid. The two NYCDP regulars commiserated with me.

Soon after, I quit for the season, returned to Cornell that fall, and nothing more came of the incident.

I dodged a bullet, probably in more ways than one, that summer.

An April Fools complimentary subway cup? Do <u>not</u> bring this *meshuggeneh kop* to the train as a guide. Compare with real stops around the Bay Parkway station on the *West End line* (*D Train*, page 74). My *West End* Bay Parkway crosses 86th Street. Yes, there is a *Sea Beach (N Train)* Bay Parkway, crossed by West 7th Street, about 14 blocks North. That was Elliott Gould's Bay Parkway. We claim that hallowed intersection for Bensonhurst as well. Mapleton? No way.

Chapter Ten

• • •

THE WEST END LINE
(forever)

The West End Line of New York City Transit:
My school bus, my ride to Coney Island,
to places far from my humble remit,
beyond my South Brooklyn ex-marshland:
   Twin silvery snakes
slither through dark abandoned catacombs
rise to squeal at rooftops of humble homes
to hiss into hot kitchens, entwine clotheslines,
then soar, winged serpents o'er river and skylines
to burrow back under the Manhattan borough
delivering me to an education thorough

    The following elevated Brooklyn West End stations were the major ones of my youth, and of Salvatore La Puma's *Boys of Bensonhurst*. Sal focused on his neighborhood's 79th Street,

I on Bay Parkway, and we both cherished Coney Island (and Sheepshead Bay next door).

- **79th Street (and New Utrecht Avenue)**: La Puma's stop
- 18th Avenue (and New Utrecht Avenue)
- 20th Avenue (and 86th Street)
- **Bay Parkway** (and 86th Street): Polacco's stop
- 25th Avenue (and 86th Street)
- Bay 50th Street (and Stillwell Avenue)
- **Coney Island** (Stillwell Avenue, last stop, with connections to the Brighton, Sea Beach, and Culver)

The stations were also points of embarkation to more distant lands. La Puma's Bensonhurst boys took the West End from 79th Street to 42nd Street/Times Square, and then a bus to a Jersey girly show, featuring Miss Sugar Buns (*The Boys of Bensonhurst [1942]*).

I hopped fourteen stops beyond Bay Parkway (in the "To City" direction) to Manhattan's Union Square (and East 14th Street) to attend Stuyvesant High School which was accessible from the Square by a three-block walk east. It was not a boring walk.

"Hey, baby, you kinda cute."

I looked straight ahead. Those gals at the Mabel Dean Bacon HS of Nursing Annex were much more worldly than we Stuyvesant nerds. Some of my intellectually precocious classmates seemed prepubertal to me.

"Hi," was the most I could muster.

"Why doncha come over heah and tawk to me?"

I walked faster. Mabel Dean is no longer there (on East 15th Street, or so). Indeed, it is no longer. I should look for a sidewalk plaque commemorating the ladies' welcoming committee. Before its demise, Mabel Dean Bacon even accepted boys, poor guys, before it moved into my old Stuyvesant HS building (345 East

15th Street) for its last incarnation. In those early days, it did not fully dawn on me that young ladies, not just boys, had a sex drive.

I lived a block from the stairs leading up to the Bay Parkway station. I know that Salvatore would agree that I did not even have to look out the train window to view New Utrecht High between 79th and 80th Streets to know I was close to returning home from Manhattan: the Italian and Jewish faces in my car told me so. Please don't ask me to describe the differences—I have been identified as Jewish by both Italians and Jews. (A sweet Yiddisher lady who usually greeted me on my newspaper route finally asked if I was Jewish. When I nodded a "no," she said, "That's OK, we're all the same.") Recall that Edward G "Rabbi's Son" Robinson played Italian bad guys (*Gravesend Bay [1940]*). Mamma often dragged me to the Jewish clothiers on the south side of 86th Street, between Bay Parkway and Bay 29th Streets. A Jewish haberdasher once told me I had "the look." Joey Irpino heard the same thing from a tailor in Kaufman's on 86th, "You have the face that could be Jewish" (*Wear It in Good Health [1943]*).

I spent a lot of time "on the train." Time that does not count waiting and walking between connections or the inscrutable, infuriating stoppages/stalls (often just before my stop, and with a burgeoning bladder). Just three years of normal two-way commutes to high school add up to more than five unbroken twenty-four-hour days on the train (conservatively 45 min/trip). Add to that total the time taking the train to our high school football and baseball games—the Bronx was far—or to social get-togethers, Madison Square Garden, Ebbets Field, Shea Stadium (Mets and Jets), Yankee Stadium, Polo Grounds (Mets and AFL football Titans), Coney Island, Sunset Pool, or just taking in the wonders of Manhattan, including surreptitious Saturday winter football "tryouts" in Central Park.

My trek to visit my football and baseball teammate, Randy Zimmerman, usually involved getting lost on the way to his upper reaches in the Bronx. I recently asked Randy the name of his neighborhood that seemed to be just south of Canada. He got back to me:

"You were right, Joe! Basically, Baychester and Pelham Bay, almost as far north as Quebec. If you made it here more often, you'd have felt at home. It [the neighborhood] was mostly Italian, six Jamaicans, a handful of Protestants, and one crazy Jew! Love, Zimmerman."

I tried to make good use of my subway commute to school, for instance, by prepping for a chemistry achievement exam from a Barron's review book. (My parents splurging on achievement test coaching sessions? *Geddouda heah*, in the local dialect.) On the Bay Parkway platform, I had Arthur Murray steps down pat:

- Stand firm at the (not obvious) spot of a specific right-hand sliding door.

- When train stops, as doors open, take two long steps, L, R, into the car.

- Right leg lateral step to the right.

- Drop ass on seat.

That seat was usually empty, and my head was buried in the Barron's book until my stop. My cerebral homing center conditioned me to raise my head as we pulled into 14th Street. (I made exceptions for some of the earlier arriving Catholic high school girls.)

Those were the waning days of New York newspapers, but among the survivors were: *Daily News, Daily Mirror, NY Post, NY Times, Herald-Tribune, World Telegram & Sun, Journal-American.* Mixed in with the English-language offerings were *Il Progresso, The Jewish Daily Forward, El Diario,* and at least one Asian daily. Origami may be a Japanese art, but most occidental folks were black belts at folding the *NY Times* so that only the pertinent article was in view. I was amazed that neighbors were not page-lashed during a reader's quest for the article continued on page 17.

You can't travel that much on the NYC transit system without getting into an occasional jam. I came home late from a date at the now defunct Cornell Nursing School (East 70's, Manhattan) and got into our store without setting off the alarm or waking Mamma, all good. She was sleeping facedown over folded arms at our kitchen table behind the store. I tiptoed past her and jumped into the bed I shared with Michael. Mamma woke up a couple of hours later, in a panic, until she saw me asleep in our room. What we put our mothers through! Earlier in the evening she was probably alerted by the rumbling of every "From City" train, and awaited my arrival a few minutes later, until she just passed out bereft of hope.

We did not have cell phones but *Joe, not for nuttin', once in a while ya coulda splurged a dime on a pay phone for your motha. Whaddya dink? Madonna!*

On one trip home from Stuyvesant, I needed to run an errand in downtown Brooklyn. I realized I had no car fare to get back on the train. Though I had jumped the turnstile on other occasions, a good opportunity did not present itself. I explained my situation to a transit policeman, and his look said, "tough shit." So, I walked, a lot. Getting to the elevated part of the West End helped me arrive home, even with my poor navigational skills. On

New Utrecht Avenue, I peered into a "coed" hangout near New Utrecht High—yes, I realized what I was missing. The ghost of La Puma was there, but not Sal. He was in Westchester by this time.

Oh, there were other golden memories:

- Since our lower Manhattan football practices went well beyond rush hour, the subway got me home later in the evening during the fall season and spring practices. We were further delayed by getting from our practice field on the East River (near Houston Street, across the river from the Williamsburg Brooklyn Domino Sugar Refinery) to the closest station. As I entered our store on one memorable evening, the alarm was ringing longer than it normally took me to negotiate the door with my gear. This told Mamma that I was hurt, and I was. I bruised a rib at practice, and I was moving slowly. Stepdad followed up this realization with his pronouncement:

  "I'm not paying no doctor's bills."

  He had a point, there should have been medical insurance for the players. In any case, I healed fast and played the next game.

- At the Union Square station after school, usually meek Stuyvesant students would grab a classmate's slide rule and play keep-away. (Slide rule? Try calculating square roots on *that*.) It was often tossed down to the tracks. Now came a test of manhood. I jumped down into the train well to grab mine and scramble back up on the platform, acutely aware of any approaching lights. No one threatened to step on white knuckles, at least not that I recall. And my schoolmates were considerate enough to drop the slide rule well away from the third rail.

- December 16, 1960, was not so golden. It was Black Friday—two airliners collided over Brooklyn. One fell in Park Slope, Brooklyn, the other at a military field in Staten Island. The combined 128 passengers on both planes perished, plus six on the ground in Brooklyn. I am not sure I attended Stuyvesant on that day so close to the holiday break, but I recall being on the train, which was a moving cavern of morose New Yorkers.

- On a spring day during senior year (1962), and feeling cocky, my buddies and I were a little too rambunctious on the train, using the poles and straps as gymnastics props, among other recreational activities. I did not think we were being a public hazard, a nuisance maybe. As we exited at Bay Parkway, a fellow traveler in civvies identified himself as a police official, took our names and addresses, and wrote letters to our parents. Stepdad made his displeasure known, physically. (Makes me wonder if I have a rap sheet. Pun intended.)

- Paying homage to Salvatore, I need to mention a citadel of Southern Italian culture, right under the West End el in Bensonhurst. Pastosa Ravioli is still there, at 74th Street and New Utrecht Avenue. Not only has it survived the flight of Italian residents, but it has expanded to eleven stores in the Metropolitan area. In Bensonhurst, people still form a queue down 74th Street for its unsurpassable ravioli for Easter Sunday. Pastosa offers a wide variety of cheeses (provolone, romano pecorino, parmigiano, etc.), salumeria (prosciutto, capocollo, sopressatta, and other salt-cured pork items), prepared dishes—its seafood salad is to die for—and now extends its "ethnic" offerings to other cultures. Just get off at 79th Street and walk in the "From City" direction about three blocks to work up an appetite.

- The other citadel, I am afraid, is now only a historical ruin, along with its contemporaries. The Cotillion Terrace (7311 18th Avenue) was the *de rigueur* place for weddings, graduations, a kind of Italian American debutante ballroom, a venue to celebrate prosperity in the new country. After a long-neglected senescence it is now a Chinese American senior center. RIP, along with the Oriental Manor and others. In its heyday, the Terrace was charmingly "overdone," or "too gavoonish" for some. (Think of early *Godfather*.) *Gavoon* is street dialect, from *cafone*, or peasant, rustic boor.

- Sal must have been thinking of the Cotillion Terrace when he invoked the upstairs Paradise Ballroom where Vito Conti, Mike Bernelli, and Guido Trapani crashed a wedding reception and fell in love with a couple of the celebrants (*The Jilted Groom [1940]*). Oh, yes, Sal, I recall "The Sandwich Toss" at these celebrations. This recent incarnation of the Olympian discus event entertained young adolescents, and it came in handy for older folks: "Hey, *guaglione* (youngster), airmail me a prosciutto and provolone, willya?"

And let us not forget the gossamer-draped swan boats bearing endless cargos of Jordan Almonds.

Chapter Eleven

• • •

WELCOME TO DIXIE
(1964)

Jim Crow's image in the land of cotton
Emblazoned on me was not forgotten
Yet, South through North, East Coast USA
Racist acts and concepts were holding sway

The South showed evidence galore
Of its racist presence hard to ignore
Yet I do not give it all the blame
The North plays its own racist game

I made a big jump from the West End of Bensonhurst. So did Sal La Puma. After all, he must have written *The Boys of Bensonhurst* while living in California. My point is that this boy can leave Bensonhurst, but the old neighborhood imbues my worldview, even into late manhood.

I had never ventured much beyond Brooklyn and Manhattan in my teens. An exception was Las Vegas in summer 1962. At thirteen, I attended a 1957 Jehovah's Witness regional convention in Baltimore. (More than spiritual inspiration, I was thrilled that it took place in the old Baltimore Memorial Stadium, home of the baseball Orioles.) In high school, I made visits to my buddy Randy Zimmerman's summer place in the Catskills ("Sour Cream Sierra," "Borscht Belt," "Jewish Alps," developed by *Kaplan's Alpen?* [naaah]) about eighty-five miles north of Randy's Bronx home— which, as I have mentioned, already seemed to me to be just south of the Canadian border.

I became an international traveler in the summer of 1964. But as I made my way out to Central America, my own country seemed, at times, to be foreign as well. My mode of travel was "by the thumb," counting on the kindness of strangers, their curiosity, or their urge to express an opinion.

I was accepted by "Cornell-in-Honduras and Guatemala," a community development project cosponsored by Cornell United Religious Work and Rotary Clubs, International. The nonsectarian project sent teams of students to live eight weeks in Central American villages, one *invited* team per village. In Ithaca, we trained on and off campus. We learned to take our prophylactic antimalarial quinine pills, as well as how to kill, pluck, and clean a chicken, operate a Coleman lantern, decontaminate suspect drinking water, set up mosquito netting, and more. We were Ivy League Boy and Girl Scouts, activities new to this Bensonhurst ingenue of both the Ivy League and the Scouts.

On retreats in the snowy woods of central New York, we delved into Central America presenting papers on rural development, land reform, the roles of the Latin American Catholic Church, indigenous cultures in Guatemala and

Honduras, among the topics I recall. We had passionate discussions on Castroism, the United Fruit Company, and US involvement in Central American internal affairs, such as the 1954 CIA-manipulated overthrow of Guatemalan President Jacobo Árbenz. Though extremely eye-opening and educational, none of it was for academic credit.

I was given two separate plane tickets: New York–Miami, and Miami–San Pedro Sula, Honduras. I cashed in the New York–Miami leg, thereby gaining spending money for Central America. The negative was that I had to negotiate the 1,500 miles or so from Ithaca, NY, to Miami. About 350 of those miles were covered by good buddy, teammate, classmate, and fraternity brother Sam Gaskins, who hailed from lovely rural Virginia, just outside DC. I accepted his lift to Great Falls, VA, from Ithaca, accompanied by another project participant, Kelly Woodbury. Now, Ms. Kelly was no shrinking violet—outspoken, fearless, a member of Cornell's ski team. She could have probably kicked my ass in an all-out fight. We agreed to hitch together from D.C. to Miami, forming a mutual protection partnership.

As we were gearing up for the DC-Miami leg, Sam's mom pulled me aside. Now, Mrs. Ceres Gaskins, president of the Virginia Women's Republicans, was confident and self-possessed. But her face of genuine concern fixed me with a somber stare.

"Take care of Kelly."

"I will, Mrs. Gaskins," I said, uncertain I was completely reassuring, or qualified.

Sam left us off on a southbound lane, a "prime" hitchhiking spot, but still about 1,100 miles from Miami. People, all males, did indeed pick us up. I'm sure Kelly was the main inducement to pull over. After Virginia came the Carolinas and palpable changes. Folks asked if we were going south to protest segregation, to "make trouble." On the official first day of that summer, June 21, three male civil rights campaigners were murdered in Mississippi—a local Black man and two, young, white Yankees. While this occurred after we reached Miami, the South we encountered was angry, if not downright scary. I knew of segregation but had never seen firsthand "triple-gender" bathrooms for men, women and *colored*. Even water fountains were racially designated for white and colored water. I suppose if their water fountain did not work, "colored" people just went thirsty until the next certified fountain.

A few drivers were memorable, like the personable young man who said something like "Them n——s are having a good time, but they know if they really act up, we can get a lot of boys up and armed." He was not the only one to make that assertion. This was 1964.

More than once, I heard the biblical justification of racism: Noah's son Ham was cast off for laughing at his nude father sleeping off a drunk. Ham became the progenitor of the Black race. Ham's brother Shem covered his father's shame, and ultimately his descendants were the white race. Somewhere along the lineages, a white, St. Louis judge made the ruling that a Black person was the equivalent of 3/5 of a white person. It's debatable whether this 1857 Dred Scott ruling was a partial "redemption of Ham."

A truck driver drove us through much of Georgia into Deland, Florida, just north of Orlando. Kelly and I took turns sleeping in the bunk behind the front seats—a mistake. He was trying to grope Kelly while I was out. She finally woke me up, and the nonsense stopped. As virtually all white Southern drivers, he was colorful, entertaining, and very pro-segregation. He was also curiously concerned for our welfare, proudly showing us off to folks along the way, "Lookee what I found!"

Then things really got weird. We were picked up soon after Deland by a white missionary family on their way to Jamaica. They were Southern Baptists intent on doing the Lord's work on the island. Reverend Dad had coordinated with a Black local pastor. I do not recall the details of their collaboration, but Dad spoke fondly of his island counterpart. Mrs. Missionary was also talkative, but their two boys were silent and unengaged, though one showed excitement when he saw a plane parked on the tarmac at a small roadside airport. What came through was that Mom and Dad defended segregation but saw no problem working with a Black preacher and his Black flock in Jamaica. Oh, yes, Kelly and I were picked up because Mom had a vision that they would rescue someone in need.

We arrived in Miami at least a couple of days before the departure of our teams to their respective Honduran villages. The ensuing events before Kelly's departure are from a *mélange* of memories. I do not pretend to recall them with accuracy, and they may bleed into each other. Importantly, Kelly would agree that Miami/Miami Beach was a serial adventure.

Our first objective was a place to sleep. One persistent cabbie drove along at our walking pace making appeals for us to hop in and shaking his head in mock worry when we didn't. What to do? For some dumb reason we took a city bus to the airport and tried to sleep on a grassy area outside a terminal—bad idea. Evening flights kept us awake, and the mosquitos were tenacious. On a city bus to Miami Beach (from the airport?), some fellow passengers found us entertaining. A lady, upon getting off, told us, "Enjoy your honeymoon." My usually quick, but also usually unthinking response was, "Hope we don't spend it all on this bus."

Back on the beach, under the stars and finally sleeping, we were awakened by a young man warning us that the police were "cleaning up" the beach. I could see them waking up people as they approached, and I did not know the consequences: a warning, a fine, jail time? "The kid" offered us refuge in "his" apartment in a nearby building, which I think was a condo. His roommate was a Cuban refugee. I do not recall the circumstances or why these two young men were together. I learned that the Jewish mother of the Cubano's girlfriend did not approve of him, but I do not recall why he was in those living quarters nor what role his young sidekick played. But we had a place to stay and a good night's sleep.

Miami was a crazy quilt of Jewish (mainly retiree), Latino, and Black residents. Before taking off for our respective Honduran villages, Kelly and I had to eat and find a better place to sleep. In the process of meeting those challenges, we got to know the crazy town better.

We wanted to cook on the beach; bad idea because it was illegal and because we had no firewood. Ahhh, a brazier-type restaurant had a cord or two of firewood near the entrance guarded by a uniformed doorman. Kelly was to distract the man, while I made off with a couple of logs. No dice. He was onto us. Famished, when coconuts would not satisfy us, we settled for lunch at a counter in a Rexall (Eckerd?) Drugs branch. I don't recall the prices, but the experience was priceless—an elderly server and his equally elderly male patron had a daily "*shtick*" whereby the poor *schlep* on the stool would ask for a menu, a piece of bread, a glass of water, etc., to go along with his meal.

"What you think, you're in the Taj Mahal? Why don't you ask for dancing girls?" the server said in a strong Yiddish accent.

The customer, in his own accent just humbly made a repeat request, looking at us for sympathy and moral support. For all I knew, this could have been a typical Litvak-Galitzianer duet from

Vaudeville or the Jewish theater in lower Manhattan. Otherwise, it would have been painful, but it became obvious that we were audience to an act, a daily one.

The second day, after the "diner" left, the counterman looked directly at us.

"You have to be firm, otherwise next thing you know they're on your side of the counter running things."

He said this with a straight face, in that accent, and I could not contain myself any longer, bursting out in laughter, which infected Kelly as well. He kept that straight face, and we rolled out of the diner into the street.

I recall another employee, perhaps the cashier, saying in her Southern accent, "Oh, they do this every day," sternly shaking her head, as if to say, *Old Yiddisher Yankee boys will be boys.*

We had encounters with others, e.g., Cuban refugees and a sporting goods store proprietor. (Kelly needed balls for her recreation specialty in Honduras. Just imagine the scene as Kelly asked how well-equipped the guy was.) We visited the Fontainebleau to use their lobby restrooms for hygiene, dental and otherwise, and for good grooming.

The second day, the kid from the beach somehow secreted us into a humble motel where I believe he was employed. He gained us access to an unoccupied room, with two naked mattresses that seemed clean. We were roused awake in the middle of the night by that same kid whose ploy was found out. He got us out and back to the Cubano. The next day, Kelly and I returned to the humble motel, and splurged, signing up for a bona fide room. I recall the proprietress looking at Kelly's Honduran flag pin and mistaking it for Israel's. Although we corrected her, we bonded, as if with our Jewish mother and mother-in-law wrapped in one.

Later the next day, Kelly hooked up with her newly arrived team in their motel. I was able to crash with her male teammates. Through a wall, I overheard Kelly exclaiming to the ladies: "Oh, Joe is SO funny!" We bid a long farewell to each other in the motel pool that night.

Yes, it is natural to ask, "What happened between you two?" Well, we got much closer. We had a blast. We got to appreciate each other under duress.

"But *really*, Joe, what happened?"

The answer is, "Not that much." I had a sense of chivalry, especially because the guy I thought was Kelly's "steady," one of her ski teammates, was also my roommate and a fraternity brother. Kelly and I dated a few times the next fall, and that was it. Besides, there were other romances that summer and after—hey, we were young.

While Kelly was on her way to Honduras, I wandered Miami lonely under my personal cloud. I called Uncle Jijjie in Vegas and took solace in that I still had two years of football eligibility. Later, I drifted into a Black neighborhood, attracted by lights under which I witnessed a night baseball game in a local league, perhaps semipro. I was impressed not only by the quality of play, but also by how engaged the community was in their young men's activities. Lots of "chatter," to be sure.

Later that night, I found myself back with the Cubano and his sidekick, but there was a third—a twentysomething dude who did not talk much. The TV showed a local news show that reported a rape-murder not far from us. A suspect was on the loose. While our new roomie was taking a shower, someone pointed out red stains on his shirt.

When the new guy finished his shower, the Cubano would not stop harassing him, getting him very agitated. I recall one beautiful question, "Where did you go to school, Penn State or . . . State *Pen*?"

"Why don't you guys leave me alone?" he shouted.

Finally, the guy couldn't take it anymore and ran out to a busy street, and the Cubano took off after him. I tried to follow the Cubano, to get him to "chill." I could see his quarry ahead looking back over his shoulder, darting through heavy pedestrian traffic. Eventually, he was gone, and I was gone as well, back to my Jewish mother at the humble motel, the next day to hook up with my team.

Epilogue to Dixie Summer of 1964. Kelly and I have reconnected. She remembers most vividly a guy offering to take us to Honduras in his boat, and that I was not too keen on the idea. As I mull this over, I recall the offer, and that I was dissuaded by jealousy and uncertainty. Also, as I think about it, the boat owner was probably the Cubano. (He must have been loaded to afford that apartment/condo.)

Kelly: [. . .] *I remember sleeping on the beach the first night (maybe two) and NOT eating at all. Not spending any money. I remember a guy who was sailing to Honduras who wanted us to go with him. We declined. I remember you breaking the "fast" with two or three hot dogs because you were just wretchedly hungry and busting open a coconut to eat that. But you had a terrible time busting through the shell.*

The Miami-Bensonhurst return trip. I hitched from Miami to Bensonhurst—no female companion. Well, I had one, from my team, but she had the presence of mind to catch public transportation from Fort Lauderdale to her New England home.

(And as I think on it, this companion may have been the one with the Honduran flag pin, and on the return trip.)

In the Deep South, I was picked up by a Black truck driver, a very personable guy who took special care of his rig. I saw a different South. All truck stops were "Black," though some had white folks running the cash register (duhhh). One commonality between Black and white truckers: They all loved their rigs and bragged about roaring down the highway like a "Boeing 707." In D.C., the driver, who was calling me "good buddy" by this time, asked me to pick up some donuts and hot coffee at a popular spot. The place was packed. All personnel and customers were Black, and then there was me. I was so tired I had trouble keeping my eyes open, and then they were met by another pair of eyes. The guy had to turn slightly askew to meet my eyes. I could not turn away, and I was so sleepy I could not soften my expression. Finally, he opened his mouth:

"That your rig out there?"

"Yeah" was all I could muster, not wanting to explain that I was a hitchhiker, and the driver was in the cab.

"Where did you start?"

"South Carolina." I mentioned the city, which I have by now forgotten.

"Man, you've come a *long* way."

"Sure have."

"Well, you be careful, now."

"Thank you, we will."

I finally made it back to Bensonhurst. Home was indeed sweet, though Mamma Vina was aghast at the weight I lost, and at some tropical rash on an ankle. My uncle Ben was visiting from L.A., and he loved that I made this trip. That I was not MIA along the way was OK with him.

This return trip lacked the sense of adventure and exploration I shared with Kelly. After witnessing Dixie racism, I was more sensitized to its Northeast version. Yes, it was there, even lurking in my own attitudes. There was one person of color in La Puma's opus, the "colored guy" in the 42nd Street Manhattan Information booth, who directed four Sicilian youths on which bus to catch to Union City, NJ (*The Boys of Bensonhurst [1942]*).

Romance on the return trip north? Between DC and NY, I was twice propositioned, by men. They took being turned down like, well, gentlemen.

THE **CANARSIE**
Hot Pastrami, Melted American Cheese, Mustard & Pickle.

2 THE **BAY RIDGE**
Honey Turkey, Swiss Cheese, Lettuce, Tomatoes, Mayo & Musta

3 THE **FLATBUSH**
Ham, Fresh Mozzarella, Roasted Peppers, Oil, Vinegar & Orega

4 THE **BENSONHURST**
Prosciutto, Capicola, Fresh Mozzarella, Roasted Peppers, Oil, Vinegar

5 THE **CAROLL GARDENS**
Sopresatta, Fresh Tomatoes, Provolone with a splash of Olive Oil.

6 THE **PARK SLOPE**
Turkey, Fresh Mozzarella, Lettuce, Tomatoes & Mayo.

7 THE **CONEY ISLAND COMBO**
Bologna, Ham, Salami with American Cheese, Lettuce, Tomatoes & M

8 THE **15th AVENUE SPECIAL**
Homemade Roast Beef with Fresh Mozzarella Topped with Fresh Tomato

9 THE **STEEPLE CHASE PARK**
Our Homemade Virginia Ham with Imported Swiss Cheese, Lettuce, Tomatoes, Mayo & M

Above: **Brooklyn is full of heroes,** though beware of baloney as in the Coney Island Combo. I almost did not live up to Bensonhurst's bold spicy combo of prosciutto, capicola (capocollo), roasted peppers, and mozzarella for mild mellowing.

Right: **Jim Crow,** a scene from Durham NC.

Chapter Twelve

• • •

STORIES ABOUT GROWING UP
(ca. 1965)

Inspired, soaring mother eagle of maturation
Well above the circling vulture of senescence
May their flights cross only at the eagle's insistence
To impart final fiery spirit to a life's duration

I had a lot to learn in college. I had just escaped Brooklyn, and though I spent a summer in Vegas before my freshman year, that wasn't enough time to make me worldly. In college, I learned that not everyone was Italian, or Jewish, or some other proper "ethnicity" (I still dislike that word) who lived on their own proper neighborhood reservation.

Part of my education was meeting a young man on the football field. He was one year behind me, tall, coordinated, lithe, a great athlete who usually made me look stupid as I tried to pass block to protect my quarterback. Bob Hudak was the son of a first-generation Hungarian father and a second-generation

German mom, a great lady. He grew up in the Finger Lakes region of upstate NY, a beautiful area full of freshwater teeming with fish. And Bob was a great fisherman. Now, I had done some saltwater fishing and crabbing, usually in Gravesend Bay off the promenade along Brooklyn's Belt Parkway. So, I had reeled in a few in my young life. But freshwater fishing was new to me. How different could it be?

I soon learned. One day, on a visit to his family, I went off with Bob to fish. He was catching everything: bass, catfish, sunfish, etc., and I'm catching nothing (well, *bubkas* fish they would say in Bensonhurst).

"Joe, you're presenting your lure the wrong way."

I countered something to the effect, "Hey, don't take me for a *chooch* (Southern Italian street dialect for *ciuccio*—donkey, ignoramus, bumpkin.) You're probably standing on the best spot in the whole lake, and you got me in some kinda black hole."

He gave me that smile out of *Esquire* and challenged me to exchange gear and location with him. So, he was using my gear on my original spot. First cast, he reeled in a bass.

"Hey, Joe, look what I got!"

This went on for a while. Final score, 15–1, in favor of Bob, and I think mine jumped on my hook out of sympathy.

Bob laughed all the way back to his home. I was disgruntled—not the word I used. He loved getting me riled up.

"Hey, Dago, there's more to the world than standing on a Brooklyn corner singing love songs to the *goils*."

Yes, an insensitive ethnic slur, but I always called him "Hunkey," a play on his Hudak last name and his Hungarian roots, before I realized that "Honkey" was Black folks' derisive name for Whitey—the wrong kind of Whitey.

Bob was not only a superb fisherman, but also an insect collector, though for this I think he counted too much on family ties. His family had connections to the 1956 Hungarian uprising against the Soviets, barely ten years before. They harbored an escapee (a Dr. "Pup") who was the curator of insects at a Hungarian natural history institution. Somehow, the refugee curator managed to secrete a huge insect collection (or a collection of huge insects) out of Hungary. He bestowed some of its prime specimens on Bob. Now I'm talking spectacular Ajax beetles bigger than a papaya, huge night-flying moths, iridescent Morpho butterflies. Bob loved to show off his specimens. Mostly he loved seeing me go iridescent green with envy.

So, it was not enough that Bob made me look stupid on the football field, that his insect collection made mine look like carpet pests, and that he had a mystical mastery over bass and other freshwater fish. He also usually came away with the prize catch when we went bird-dogging at all-female schools surrounding Ithaca.

Despite it all, we were good buddies, and that's what buddies do, especially at that age—get on each other's nerves. Bob did respect me. For one thing, I was tenacious in academics, and not usually as frustrated as I was on the gridiron. At a recent reunion, Bob told my Nancy, "Joe is one of the toughest guys I came across on the field." So, we're still buddies and have crossed paths several times over the fifty-seven years since graduation (Chapter Twenty-Five). And I am always thankful that his lies put me in a good light.

Bob runs a successful plant bio-stimulant business for growers worldwide, and he bestowed upon me a couple of small research grants at MU to check out possible components (all *natural* compounds, BTW). He is now marketing his own brand internationally with those components. One of his two sons is VP. (And he just made Bob a grandfather, September 24, 2022.)

Bob's family touched me and mine over the years, and not a single member of his family came from the Italian peninsula. I can't be certain of that, though: When the Huns sacked Rome they may have left a few genes whose descendants now reside in Bob's genome (and mine?).

Origin of "Polacco." So, do I have Eastern European genes? I was told by a Cuban friend that on the island, *polaco* meant "Jew." Not so unusual. I was asked by a professor of Italian at the University of Missouri if I were Jewish: Italian surnames, such as Polacco, Albanese, Tedesco, Franco, Russo, et *al.*, signify founding immigrants from Poland, Albania, Germany, France, Russia, etc., and a good number of those immigrants could have been Jews escaping persecution by shedding their original surnames.

Whereas "Sicilian" covers an island of patchwork ethnicities, individual ethnicity is often identified by sub-regions of origin. For instance, in Uruguay, as Nancy tells and I witnessed, Spaniards are *gallegos* (from Galicia, in the Spanish northwest). In Brooklyn, Middle Eastern Jews (*Mizrahim*), as opposed to the European Ashkenazim, were "Syrian Jews." The Polacco-Jewish link is especially intriguing to me. Argentine postdoc Ariel Goldraij, Jewish himself, maintained that *polaco* not only meant Jewish, but an itinerant Jew peddling haberdashery. I knew at least one in Bensonhurst, an opera buff who often did a street duet with Mamma in front of our linoleum store. (*La Boheme* brought tears to Abe's eyes.) Baseball old-timer Joe Garagiola described such *landsmen* in the St. Louis Italian Hill section.

Science can put such intriguing speculations to bed—my genome contains little or no Ashkenazi or Mizrahi sequences, but reflects the littoral of the Mediterranean, from Greece to Spain/North Africa, with the major contributions from the Italian peninsula. I do not mind being "misidentified" as Jewish. I take it as a compliment. Over- and undervaluing 'racial' sequences often has disastrously tragic consequences. It's not what your genome *is*, it's what you *do* with it.

A good buddy saved my life. Sam Gaskins is now retired from a rewarding career as a doc of family medicine. However, he hit some rough patches at Cornell, very little of it his fault. He sought something adventurous, out of his normal life in the verdant Virginia hills near DC. So, just before Christmas break in our Cornell junior year (December 1964), we decided to visit Uncle Jijjie in Vegas. I believe we warned Uncle Jijjie that we were coming.

The idea was to hitch from Ithaca, NY, to Las Vegas, NV, in late December, a trek that involved crossing the Rockies—yes, an idea, but not a very good one. Serendipity saved us more than once. I was still asleep on the morning before our departure, and Sam came running into a communal "barracks" at the fraternity house, holding the Cornell *Daily Sun*. There was an ad that I paraphrase as "deliver car to Denver [from Ithaca]." A phone call was made, and Sam was given the keys, credit cards for gas, and a drop-off address in Denver. Amazing trust was involved.

The trip started off uneventfully. We left snowy western New York State eventually dropping down to Champaign-Urbana, Illinois, to spend a day at Sam's sister's place. A bright sun came up that first morning as we drove into Illinois. It revealed a flat, boring, and charmless Midwest, with corn stubble sticking through a layer of snow, under the frigid, forlorn gazes of corn silos. Sis lived with her husband and young child. Dad was a professor of mathematics and was intrigued by our itinerary. His logical mind worked out the best routes west. This was well before geo-stationary satellite imaging and Google Maps. All planning was on folded paper road maps. Still, we were much better off than Columbus.

So, off we went continuing our westward migration. I had no driver's license, and Sam was getting sleepy doing all the driving (though, as I recently learned, his brother-in-law had slipped him some "speed"). On one stretch there was virtually no traffic, an opportunity for an unlicensed driver to take the wheel.

"Hey, Joe. This car is automatic. Here's the steering wheel, and the two pedals are for the gas and brake. Even you could figure this out, like the bumper cars in Coney Island."

I got behind the wheel. The plan was to stay on an east-west two-lane road, numbered in the 60s as I recall. Sam was trying to sleep in the front passenger seat, and periodically I would scream "Sam!" to rouse him up. Yes, young guys know how to bond while having a good time.

One memory is indelible: We stopped to get gas and refreshments at a honkey-tonk in southern Missouri. The place was hopping, and the jukebox blared "Give Me Forty Acres to Turn This Heap Around." I just googled it, no kidding. It was a 1964 one-hit wonder by the Willis Brothers, which squares well with our December 1964 trek out west. Folks in the place looked at us two Northeast college greenies like we dropped down from a spacecraft. At least Sam had the accent, kinda. We forged on.

We were moving along, and I was getting the feel for driving, even feeling cocky, until I realized I was on the wrong road—the first of many wrong turns, metaphorical or otherwise, but I've made it this far to tell the story. Sam did not believe me when

I woke him but confronted with the road sign, he took it as a Teachable Moment.

"Joe, this is how you do a road turn."

I was to make sure I was on an empty straight stretch, and the trick was to pull over to the right, turn the front wheels left, move forward, stop, turn wheels right and back up.

"Now you're going to learn a new gear, reverse, and this will be on your road test for your license, if you ever get one."

I don't know if I was giddy from lack of sleep or not paying enough attention, but when I went forward, with the wheels turned left, I gunned it, and the car was stuck fast in a frozen embankment, front wheels suspended above the gully. I needed those forty acres, and somehow, I found reason to laugh. Sam was appalled.

There was no way we could dislodge the car. I recall at least one good Samaritan stopping to offer help, and then a state trooper showed up. He assessed our situation and flagged down a few passersby. I could not claim I was the driver, so the ignominy of getting into that predicament fell on Sam.

Finally, a fellow with a powerful pickup truck and a strong rope was able to get us back on the shoulder of the road. We thanked good Samaritan number two, and then the trooper turned to Sam.

"How long you say you been driving, son?" It was a pointed question directed at Sam's incompetence. I don't recall Sam's response, but I believe he said something like four years.

The trooper got serious. "I'll need to see identification, registration, and why you're in Missouri."

I had a Cornell ID and a Social Security card. I gave my 86th Street Bensonhurst address. Sam had his driver's license with his Virginia address, but the car had Minnesota plates, and we were stuck in Missouri on our way to Colorado. I do not recall if we produced a registration, but in any case, it did not look good for us.

"I'm going to have to take you boys in for questioning." He dropped those words on us like a sledgehammer. Then Sam got an inspiration and produced a note from the glove compartment: "Deliver car to [address in Denver]." Somehow, this convinced the trooper to let us go on our way, but the car would not budge. The trooper put his arm through the window and released the parking brake. "How long you say you been driving?"

This repeat question inflicted so much shame on Sam, I was afraid he'd point to me as the culprit. But, no, he took it like a man. I knew I would pay for his pain.

Back on the road, and I do not recall if I got behind the wheel again. We dealt with the rest of Missouri, and all five-hundred boring miles of Kansas and eastern Colorado to the Denver area. Road conditions were OK, no snow that I recall. Our hopes were raised by the apparently affluent surroundings of our destination. We fantasized that we would be put up for the night, maybe given a meal, or a gratuity, but no. We showed up, and a very dignified African American man was in front, dealing with a bunch of beagles, or hunting dogs as they seemed to me. He was happy to see us.

"Well, thank you very much!" he greeted us, and went inside to call his boss.

Sam and I looked at each other, with hope in our hearts.

"Mr. _____ thanks you. So, you've come a long way from Ithaca. Where to now?"

"Las Vegas."

"How are you getting there?"

"We're hitching."

I clearly remember his retort, "Well, you have a hitch that is a hitch." My heart sank, but he dropped us off at a good roadside spot.

We were now faced with two new problems: Colorado had apparently declared war on hitchhiking, and in the early '60s, a burglary ring was exposed in the Denver Police Department. So, in our sleep-deprived paranoid state, we were dealing with an unfriendly, and possibly untrustworthy, police department. We tried to hitch clandestinely by hiding from traffic and approaching cars stopped at a light or stop sign. All we did was scare folks, and luckily the police were not called. Cell phones would have done us in.

The ploy did work when we were picked up by three or four young ladies, out on a Saturday night adventure. One asked, "Are you guys running from the law?" Apparently, our answer was either too tame or too threatening, and we were left off. We did make it out of Denver and into the lonely Rockies. A fellow who seemed in retrospect to have antisocial tendencies left us off in the middle of nowhere, at the bottom of a long incline, the only evidence of civilization (besides the road and the rare passing car), a roadside gas station closed for the night. It was freezing, and as usual I was not dressed for the very cold weather. We could see headlights illuminating the night sky, and then a car making its downhill descent, going so fast as it passed we could not even be sure we were seen. (Yes, a flashlight would have helped.) In desperation, we tried to hitch in either direction—no go. I made a trek to that gas station, perhaps to find warmth in the bathroom. Everything was locked. I trekked back to Sam.

"This is bullshit! I'm freezing." I trudged down to the culvert separating the four lanes and tried to sleep—bad move. I am not sure if I fell asleep, but was roused by Sam screaming, "Joe, we have a ride!" A trucker, bless his heart, picked us up, and he was going our way. Maybe he saw my body in the culvert—but I'm taking no credit for being a wimp. I believe Sam saved me from freezing to death that night.

> We have long lifetimes on this sphere
> I have time to be my life's gazetteer
> Yet also time to make fatal mistakes
> Except for friends who hit my brakes

The rest of the trip was much more exciting than Kansas. We skirted Las Vegas—the one in New Mexico. At one stop, a young lady serving behind a diner counter seemed interested in joining us—though its scenery was lovely, her town looked otherwise boring. We did spend a lot of precious daylight and energy there: As we stationed ourselves to put our thumbs out, I picked up a flat rock and threw an underhanded riser at a small sign across the road. The sign was no bigger than home plate—direct hit. Sam moaned a guttural curse, and the contest was on. Though I was successful on the first try, neither of us could duplicate that marksmanship.

We were saved from throwing our arms out by two young *chicanos* who offered us a ride. They were very courteous, and introduced themselves, probably looking forward to learning our story. Sam and I made a pact to stay awake to keep our guard up—yes, inexcusable racism on our part. In an apparent instant, we were being shaken awake from deep slumber. The two gentlemen left us at a town that looked like a Western movie set. (I want to say that town was Cimarron, but details are blurred.) There was a large wooden sign with "BANK" in big red letters over an establishment. I believe that a woman picked us up, so unusual, but Sam and I must have looked harmless—thoroughly road-beaten. The last driver was a guy looking for an escape. We convinced him to drive into Las Vegas, the one in Nevada. On the way, we stopped at an overlook of Hoover Dam and, as if on cue, three young men urinated into the nighttime hissing abyss.

Las Vegas was Sam's introduction to my Uncle Jijjie and my Chicago cousin, Johnny, who was in Vegas at the time. Johnny was, and is, a sweet guy, but he could have been cast for *Casino* (Martin Scorsese, director, 1995). Both Jijjie and John took a real shine to Sam—such differences in age, accents, height, and experience. Uncle Jijjie's home was a meeting place for Vegas personalities, most of them Brooklyn ex-pats. Picture a Virginia college guy getting along with Sal La Puma's Bensonhurst Boys, but Sam came through.

Sam and I did venture out to sample Vegas. We hit a couple of casinos and The Nashville Nevadan (The Nashville Nevada Club according to the internet), country music in the desert. It was a far cry from that Missouri honky-tonk. Yes, the music was live. And, yes, it had a bar and dancing, but flanking the band and circling the dance floor were individual show windows each featuring a live, long-legged lady sitting by a phone. She could be reached by any phone located at individual tables and along the bar. Most of the ladies seemed to be on the phone. (Much later I saw similar setups in the redlight districts of Amsterdam and Hamburg, though I hesitate to draw any further parallels.) Sam and I did not stay very long, convincing each other we were not country music types and that we would not be seen dead on the dance floor with those yokels. Recall that this was December 1964, well before Vegas became even more tawdry.

Our experience was akin to La Puma's four young men in Union City, NJ—Frankie, oldest at seventeen, Nick the altar boy, Rocco the boxer, and Gene the wild drummer and youngest at fifteen (*The Boys of Bensonhurst [1942]*). They were dazzled by the street action, and girlie shows, but eventually were disappointed, and they made their way back to Bensonhurst. They did not have to travel cross-country; they merely backtracked via bus to Times Square and the West End to 79th Street.

Overall, though, Sam's odyssey got him what he bargained for—a virtually complete break from a broken, long-standing, romantic relationship back home in Virginia.

Our way back to Ithaca? Ahh, here providence (and Sam, again) came to our aid. There was yet another local ad in an Ithaca newspaper, or perhaps on the "ride board" at a student union. Two Ithaca College students sought someone to share driving and expenses from Albuquerque to Ithaca. This was arranged before our trip West. Sam and I celebrated New Year's Eve on an overnight Vegas-Albuquerque Greyhound. At the magical hour, booze was passed around. A couple behind us made each other's acquaintance, pure serendipity, and I turned around to take a flash photo of them. I bet I can find it given enough time—a handsome young couple with shocked, wide-eyed expressions. The crap I got away with still amazes me.

The two Ithaca College students, a guy and a gal, waiting at the Albuquerque bus depot were prepared not to like us two Cornell guys, but by the time we pulled into Ithaca, we four were good buddies.

Chapter Thirteen

• • •

HONDURAS, TWO SUMMER LANDINGS
(1964, 1966)

'Tis so easy to live in a sheltered home
And obsess on trivia, a common syndrome
Daresay we need call at our neighbors' door
Their problems are ours and not to ignore

And once we're joined in a common space
They can offer love, sweet inspiration
Love that binds, beyond prejudice and race
And that helps us in our own tribulation

I did two eight-week summer stints in Honduras in community development projects with fellow Cornell students. Honduras for me was many things, most borne out as a tale of two villages.

Cofradía, the 1964 village, was *developed*, to the extent that it had electricity for a few hours a day and running water, albeit with a high coliform count. It had a rudimentary town square

105

and a charmingly rustic wooden movie house that also hosted live presentations. We celebrated the Fourth of July in the square. Cofradía provided the sound system and a DJ. The crowd went nuts to Carolyn Heiser's baton-twirling routine. The DJ moved his mic down the row of gringos singing their Star-Spangled Banner. I was the last, and the crowd laughed uproariously at my rendition. I wasn't even trying to be funny.

Closer to the end of our stay, the movie house was the scene of the celebration of our collaboration with townsfolk in a Honduran "cultural review." For some numbers, we gringos wore traditional peasant garb, tailored to our measurements, as we pranced to "Bombas," Central American verse and dance to typical boy-girl picaresque confrontations. The double entendre abounded, the material never got old judging from the crowd response. "El Sacrificio Maya" was a Mayan human sacrifice scene in which I played a god, cross-legged in loin cloth, receiving the offering of a beautiful maiden, and trying to keep a straight face as the school principal/high priest, with his back to the audience, looked me in the eye and licked his chops in anticipation.

Cofradía was a bittersweet, bracing, basic experience—where the exposed nerves and the precarious condition of many people were all too obvious, but where the mere presence of young gringos was a *cause célèbre*. We spiced up life, providing a close-up glimpse of another world. Town kids peered at us nightly through every crack and open window in our quarters. They were transfixed, as if watching television.

Cofradía awoke our own humanity. Through our health surveys, one-on-one literacy teaching, and construction projects, we identified with the daily struggles of many. We interacted with a traveling Alliance for Progress medical triumvirate—a doctor, nurse and Charlie the latrine guy (a role not to be denigrated).

We connected with folks at basic levels, but we also had *fun*. Sundays were often spent on a beautiful river, or the Caribbean beach at/near Omoa. (Thank you for adopting us, Nelly Duarte.) The last week of going-away parties made our departure an emotional catharsis.

I should not leave a discussion of Cofradía without mention of our patient and charming team leader, Billie Schildkraut. Guillermina, as she was called, dealt with my infantile outbursts and kept the team together and on task. She was also a guitar virtuoso. Over the summer, several young Honduran men came by to join her in musical duets or trios.

I retain the friendship of a young *cofradireño*, José Hernan Ayala. He grew from an active, curious, and aspiring ten-year-old in 1964 to a successful businessman today. Nancy and I spent Thanksgiving 2018 with José, his Rosa and family, on their *finca* near Tegucigalpa.

In summer of '64 I went to Honduras with one pair of shoes, sneakers, and I soon walked out of them. José's dad, the town shoemaker, made me a new pair of fine leather shoes. That very much touched me. (Villagers may have seen me as the "poor boy" of the team, the guy with only one pair of shoes, and no camera. In truth, I was just a poor planner.)

Writing these accounts has given this seventy-eight-year-old flashbacks (but probably not enough). In summer 1964, we were in the major general store of Cofradía, run by an enterprising Lebanese-Honduran family. The news of the Gulf of Tonkin incident had come over his radio. My response, intemperate and reactive as usual, was that we should "punish" whoever was responsible. My opinion very much had changed a few years later in graduate school, in the "man-child phase" of my story (Chapter Sixteen).

Left: Don José Ayala, ca. 10-years-old (1964, Cofradía), with his sisters Delmis and Lourdes and their mother Vina—yes, his Mamá and my Mamma were "tocayas," sharing the same first name.

Right: José (Chepito) and Rosa and four grand-kids on their finca near Tegucigalpa (ca. 2022). Don José is not only a successful businessman and grower, but has long been a benefactor of Honduran agriculture through the Zamorano Ag school, and other charities and outreach activities. (Check out the boots; Don José's dad was a shoemaker who made me a pair of shoes in 1964.)

Chiquila, 1966. Ahh, Chiquila provoked emotions so different from Cofradía, much more tending to gloom and melancholy, and American military adventures in Indochina did little to buoy our team spirits. I caught a "premonition" linking Indochina and Chiquila while in the major town of San Pedro Sula, readying the supply truck for our trip to the village. I was sweating heavily, making multiple trips to the truck, while a trim, thirtyish fellow in the lobby of our hotel was reading a newspaper and also following my movements. He had Italian features and a full head of beautiful wavy black hair. Finally, he asked me what I was doing. He even asked me in Italian, for which I was not too useful. I explained the concept of community development, winning people's hearts while helping them move out of poverty. He told me that he was with the US military, and "when you fail, we'll move in."

"We won't fail." I expressed indignantly. I got a wry smile as he wished me good luck.

I could only conjecture what roles he had played or was about to. US-backed counterinsurgencies come to mind (See, for example, *School of the Americas: Military Training and Political Violence in the Americas.* Lesley Gil, Duke University Press, 2004).

Compared to Cofradía, Chiquila was *undeveloped*—a depressing reversion to a third world backwater. Not even bus drivers knew the exact location of Chiquila. We would instruct the driver to let us off at a nondescript edge of an unpaved main road. From there we found the path that wended its way to a village that had *nada*, nothing, neither running water nor electricity, with hope in the shortest supply.

Chiquila hadn't had a party for many years.

"When do you have parties?" I asked a young lady. (Cofradía always had parties.)

Contrasts between Cofradía (1964) and Chiquila (1966, page 116).
Above is Cofradia's "Comedor Infantil" (children's breakfast center)
during construction, when we were caught in a sudden tropical
rainstorm. Seven of our team's ten are in the photo, Billie Schildkraut is third from right. Right: Inauguration of the breakfast program. A local producer (Leche Sula) provided milk and cereal daily.

"Well, I don't remember a party, but Mamá told me that the last party ended in a machete fight, and someone was killed."

Except for a few enterprising folks and leaders, *chiquileños* appeared to be "whipped." Residents "crashed" in Chiquila on the way to something better, or maybe it was their penultimate stop to nothing.

The *Padres de Familia* committee, a group of leaders, was a point of light. The Padres—family heads—invited our team of Cornell students to live in Chiquila for eight weeks to engage in community development projects. We were housed in a humble one-room wooden structure. Long curtains divided the interior into thirds. Each outer third was a student dorm, four cots for the gals on one side, and cots for the four guys on the other. A middle passageway of beaten sod went from the front door to the back that opened to a covered patio where we cooked, ate, and gossiped. Latrines were further out back. A brook was close to the front door. Folks bathed and washed clothes in the brook which was also a water source for cattle upstream. Though a lovely stream, its water was not potable without treatment.

Could eight *universitarios americanos* help resuscitate a moribund village? Maybe, were it not for the military government and the bad judgment of our team leader, yours truly.

On a midsummer's night, we lingered on our back porch. We kibitzed, wrote letters, practiced steps to *cumbias* emanating from a scratchy radio. Did we sip that infernal distillate of fermented sugar cane squeeze, that firewater *aguardiente*? Whatever, there was a lapse in discipline. We left personal belongings and team equipment unsecured on the patio.

Next morning, nursing student Peggy showed up at the building site of Chiquila's new school. Peggy always looked distressed. Hey, she dealt daily with villagers' injuries, wounds, malnutrition, and parasites.

Peggy held back tears. "We were robbed. They took everything." *Familia* leader Don Carlos at her side sadly nodded affirmation.

"Holy shit!! I left my wallet on the table!" I sprinted to our house not stopping first to console Peggy, such a caring and charismatic leader I was.

They took everything not nailed down—camping stove, lanterns—*everything*. And, of course, my wallet.

As team leader, and under the thrall of machismo—much of it developed in Bensonhurst—I took immediate responsibility to walk five kilometers to inform the next town's mayor. He headed the municipality that included Chiquila. The mayor was a fatherly figure and always helpful. He had helped us garner building materials for Chiquila's school. Hearing *mi denuncia/* my complaint, he dutifully informed the local military garrison.

I should have consulted with my team first. Even coming to the same course of action, we would have all been "on the same page."

Chiquileños, upon learning of the impending "visitation" were apprehensive all day. The lone schoolteacher, a young single woman, almost gave in to panic.

After sundown, came a series of strong knocks on our front door. I opened to look out over a pattern of about thirty moonlit helmets, as if regular rows of yellow-tinted corn kernels. The platoon leader, standing on a step and looking me in the eye, announced the intention to *registrar las casas*, search the village houses for our belongings. I went off with him and a few troops. I asked why other soldiers stayed behind, but I do not recall a clear answer.

The "searching" routine was to ram a door open with rifle butts and boot heels. While soldiers forced entry, others surrounded the house, blocking escape—a military operation. Their quarry was folks still half asleep confronted with armed soldiers rifling through pitiful belongings. I was there to identify our items, but I was seen by the invaded as another pillager.

After two such searches, I told the leader that this was no way to do business, that without the villagers' trust our student mission was dead, that thieves would not keep the stash in town, and that in any case the thieves were likely outsiders. (We were observable from mysterious huts on overlooking mountain slopes.) He gave me the cold-eyed mechanical response, "We have to finish searching the houses."

His soldiers were fit and well-fed and seemed to be teenagers. They had an attitude of superiority, though many probably came from humble villages, or urban slums. They repeatedly apologized for our having to see how Hondurans lived.

¡Qué gente! What people! they commented to each other on the deplorable peasants.

Then we were marching out of town, accompanied by the "village idiot" the soldiers had corralled. No idiot he was. Rather, his bizarre behavior masked antimilitary feelings. He was ordered to provide the whereabouts of his older brother, a suspected anti-government insurrectionist, a *guerrillero*. It was clear he was leading the soldiers out of town to protect his brother.

Recognizing this ploy, a soldier uttered a contemptuous *¡hijueputa!* (sonuvabitch!), ramming the fellow's exposed chest with an upward stroke of his rifle muzzle. The poor guy ran.

The soldier leveled his rifle. "Don't shoot!" I yelled. The shot went over the guy's head, perhaps in response to my appeal. The poor fellow landed face down in a roadside gulley. Soldiers ran up and pulled him to his feet:

"I have no idea where my brother is!" He blurted this, bleeding, hysterically crying.

I knew then that the legitimacy of military government is discharged from a rifle muzzle. (Bringing home Mao's *political power from the barrel of a gun.*)

As I was repeating my sermon to the military about counterproductive actions, teammate Reeve appeared. He reinforced my appeal. Then, pulling me aside:

"The soldiers that stayed behind are beating up people. Peggy and our team are tending to the victims."

We both appealed to the soldiers, and with this the operation finally ended. They apologized yet again for the Honduras we had to witness and endure in Chiquila.

Our team reunion that night was ghostly, horrid, but we were glad to be alive and together. I felt like a dupe, a traitor, a weakling. The real heroes were Reeve, Peggy, and the rest.

The next day Chiquila was a frigid hell. One tyke, a favorite of mine, looked at me coldly:

"Yo le ví a robar"—"I saw you about to rob (us)." His was a "registered" house that I had invaded.

Yes, there *were* foci of light: After a short interval, and our many apologies, gringo-Honduran camaraderie returned to the school building site. There was indeed a bittersweet farewell party in the partially completed school. We danced to a battery-operated record player and a homemade marimba, "pieces of wood that sing with a woman's voice." (*Maderas que cantan con voz de mujer*, from *Tehuantepec* by Mexican composer/poet José Guízar Morfín, 1906–1980.) There was no machete fight.

But light is best seen on a dark background: Two sorry souls were nabbed trying to cash a grimy $65 check that had been folded and sequestered in my wallet, news that made Honduran radio. Teammate John and I confronted the suspects in a San Pedro Sula jail. We looked them in the eye, like real TV detectives.

"A stranger offered us money for cashing the check," one said.

"We are innocent," said the other.

"Who was this stranger?" I asked, yes, quite stupidly.

"He was a stranger with a mustache and said he would wait outside the bank."

They declared innocence, and in fact seemed incapable of the crime.

Then, giving us a conspiratorial look, "We are abiding hunger here." "Here" was a sunlit patio within four tall, windowless walls. Everyone in a crowd of about twenty men was standing. I did not see seats or benches. Was this their recreational break?

"We need to pay for our food."

They certainly did not look overweight. We gave them some lempiras—a few dollars—and left the prison.

John and I continued on our way; he was my new hitchhiking partner. In Mexico City, John's dad wired him money for a bus ticket back to Texas.

My benefactor was that grimy check recovered from those two poor souls. The father of another "Cornell-in-Honduras" member, from a different team, was a corporate executive in Mexico City. He cashed the check, greatly facilitating my trek north to visit Uncle Jijjie in Las Vegas. That same liberating check was the "go to jail" ticket for those two poor souls.

More darkness: Just before the Chiquila summer of 1966, our project funding from Rotary Clubs International had fallen through. A foundation came to our rescue, requesting only a report on our activities. The foundation was a CIA front. I learned I was a CIA pawn on a 1968 visit to Chiquila with my fiancée Mary Schaeffer. The news had made the Honduran airways, and the *chiquileños* were only too keen to let me know. A pattern was clearly developing around us gringos—talk about *déjà vu*.

Our Chiquila team at summer's end, 1966. To me the photo smacks of melancholy, but the school in our midst was almost completed, and was operational when Mary and I visited in 1968.

Chapter Fourteen

• • •

BOY DAZED IN THE BAYS:
GRAVESEND, CHESAPEAKE, NARRAGANSETT

(Summer, 1965)

> Water, amniotic fluid to life's cycles,
> Lubricates youthful passion and mirth,
> Induces a dance to our summer canticles
> Impelling us to our recurring re-birth
>
> Water, as well, saline base of our blood
> Need we spill it to anoint our progeny?
> And, so re-christen the primeval mud
> To advance humankind's scarlet destiny?

To graduate with a BS in biochemistry, I had to show Cornell a summer spent in a science-related activity. Neither a Las Vegas casino, a Brooklyn neighborhood park, nor a 1964 summer in Cofradía, Honduras, qualified, no matter how many insects and beetles I collected in the latter. Summer '65, before my senior year, was my last chance to graduate on time, and as usual, I lucked out, in science and in love.

(One can be lucky in love, but fortunes do change after the credits. The "happily ever after" hardly ever lasts forever, or as we say in science, "those experiments are still in progress." Happy memories do persist, though. My PhD advisor, Samson R. Gross, often prefaced conclusions drawn from his old experiments with this caveat: "Old experiments are like old girlfriends, you tend to remember only the good things.")

I came across the summer employment opportunity in a folder in the dean's outer office. An entry described research experiences in marine biology at the Chesapeake Biological Laboratories in Solomons, Maryland. A graduate advisor recommended the place. In fact, he had a love connection there, but this is my love story.

I got the job, in a field station off the main Solomons lab. I joined two other college guys lodged in a former beach house with a new lab addition. During working hours, two lab supervisors, local workers, and students joined us. But weekends and evenings usually belonged to us—the Three Maritime Musketeers.

At work we counted, measured, and weighed harvested marine specimens preserved in plastic bags of formaldehyde—this, five years before the founding of OSHA. While the effects on our pulmonary and cerebral membranes (and on our DNA) were at best side issues, our goal was overridingly worthy—to assess off-effects on estuarine ecology of thermal pollution from the cooling water discharge of a proposed nuclear power plant.

We were more than just cheap labor, however. In Solomons, we attended seminars and lab meetings, and each of us presented our individual projects. And it wasn't all work and science, either. We had fantastic beach parties with the main crew. I loved the local bars and the rural seafood joints where they dumped a large pot of steamed blue crabs over your newspaper-covered table (nutcrackers, *de rigueur).* The waters were full of clams, oysters, crabs, striped bass, eels (yes, delicious), and much more. And the air and aeries were rife with osprey, bald eagle, hawk, falcon, owl, and other raptors. Terrapins, amphibians, and invertebrates were legion in fresh and brackish waters. I was in heaven on earth (and water), and I haven't even dwelled on the spiders, beetles, and butterflies.

Amid all this social, scientific, and natural bounty, Morgan walked into my life—a new heavenly dimension. She was a star in that neck of the woods, and the girlfriend of a local football hero who had gone on to a military academy. Her family had a lovely place in the woods, a stone's throw from both the Patuxent Estuary and the Chesapeake. I said she walked in, though she was "there" from summer's beginning. I certainly had no unseemly motives and made no moves; we just fell for each other, suddenly—a midsummer's dream come true.

Our new relationship was obvious to all. One of the local guys, a handyman/technician of sorts, warned "that soldier boy's gonna kick your ass." That same local guy, looking out on the bay from high on a cliff, spied Morgan and me floating in a dinghy and yelled a greeting. I should have answered, "When does the ferry come through?"

My life is full of *shoulda saids.* Instead, I yelled, "Hey, Jim, what time is it?"

"It's time for love!" Sonuvagun, he was funny, but very annoying, and not too subtle. Yes, Jim and I were made for each other, another match made in heaven.

I had not yet acquired a driver's license, which did little to mitigate my insecurity with internal combustion engines. Getting Morgan out on the bay in that dinghy just required muscle and

DENYSE'S FERRY.
the first place at which the Hessians and British landed on Long Island Aug 22nd 1776. NOW FORT HAMILTON.

Bensonhurst is/was Bays, and Marshland. Extensive marshes gave Brooklyn its name, Breuckelen, Dutch for broken land. Stepdad's immigrant Uncle founded Pietro D'Agostino and Sons, Trucking. Their business took part in filling in Gravesend Bay marshland. They did not touch Denyse's ferry landing (near present day Fort Hamilton and the Verrazzano Bridge), where 15,000 thousand British troops came ashore from Staten Island in late August 1776 to teach the upstart new nation a lesson.

The US was baptized in mud, blood and sacrifice. To me bays and estuaries are akin to incubators of life, though I accept that oceanic volcanic vents probably were life's primordial origins.

motivation, neither of which was limiting. Yes, I could harness motor power to get our lab outboards around the estuarine waters to make "collections," such as snagging blue crabs off pilings with a long-handle net. But could I be counted upon in an emergency?

That situation arrived one Sunday afternoon when our boss, Doctor Mihursky ("Joe" to us), phoned the lab—he, his wife, their young son, and a visiting couple were stranded across the Patuxent with a dead motor. They were able to paddle to a very small town and locate a phone to call the lab. I found myself towing those five souls with a lab outboard under increasingly threatening skies. I missed the first attempt to dock them in our lab slip. On the second, they were delivered—under a fierce rain.

Joe Mihursky was good for my self-confidence, and not just because he trusted my navigational skills. I felt an affinity for this other "polacco named Joe." We both came from urban, working-class "ethnic" families in which we were among the first to attend college. I met Joe's down-to-earth parents on a collecting trip to his home waters in PA; I was part of the family. Working with Joe was akin to working with my Uncle Gregory back in Bensonhurst. With sensitivity and humor Joe advised me to use my head in the lab. For instance, this Mihursky Fable: A bird found that getting a piece of straw into a tree hole was much easier pointing it in end first, rather than holding it sideways.

Joe passed in 2018, at the age of eighty-five, after a long career as a champion and steward of estuarine environments. This from his obituary: "[Joe] Mihursky was a strong and informed voice supporting the innovative and very successful Maryland Power Plant Siting Program. His work led to the State of Maryland passing legislation protecting these ecosystems by controlling the amount of heat a power plant could discharge into estuarine waters." Good science can lead to good policy. Communicating science certainly helps. Joe communicated, without talking down.

In summer 1965, I was still schizophrenic: an accomplished Cornell junior, about to turn twenty-one, but also an insecure, unpolished Italian American kid from unromantic Bensonhurst. Whereas Maryland had the lovely and bountiful Chesapeake, my Bensonhurst could only proffer Gravesend Bay, a blasphemed body of water. The desecration started well before my birth. Salvatore La Puma (*Gravesend Bay [1940]*) wrote of "muscled men, [who steered] the tractors [that] coughed like old smokers as they pushed the bay back into the Atlantic by dumping in sandcastles and boulders at the water's edge." By 1950, my bay's beautiful marshland had been filled in to expand real estate acreage. Today, much of the bay's "shore" is buttressed by boulders draped with oil, tar, and flotsam in front of a sea wall to hold back the tides and moor the congested Belt Parkway.

But this apparent incompatibility between the Chesapeake and Gravesend was an illusion. The bays were linked, as I was with Morgan, my willowy Anglo-Saxon bellflower of the imposing cliffs over the Chesapeake. In fact, Bensonhurst and Maryland were linked in blood, from the very first days of American history—in the Battle of Brooklyn. A friend from New England (of all places) told me that "Battle of Brooklyn" conjured a food fight, a filo-falafel-focaccia fracas? Seriously, folks, the first and bloodiest battle of the Revolutionary War took place in Brooklyn—to be precise, it started in Bensonhurst. Fifteen thousand British troops from over four hundred ships came ashore at Denyse's Ferry Landing (near what is now the Verrazzano Narrows Bridge) in Gravesend Bay. It was the largest amphibious landing in history, until the world wars (think Gallipoli and Omaha Beach). The

Americans, no longer colonists but defending their sovereign nation in late August 1776, were outnumbered and badly mauled, but General Washington and his troops eventually made a miraculous escape to Manhattan to fight many other days and eventually to drain, wear down, and defeat the British.

My point is that fierce resistance by the patriots enabled Washington's escape with his troops and supplies. And much of the patriot resistance was provided by about four hundred Marylanders, under General William Alexander (Lord Stirling). At least half of that regiment perished, and the location of their remains is still unknown, but certainly near the shores of Gravesend Bay. This Maryland-Brooklyn connection, spawned in the waters of the Chesapeake and Gravesend Bays, helped give life to the American Revolution.

Another bay figured in that summer of 1965: Our lab made a trip north to Newport, Rhode Island, on the Narragansett Bay which, according to Wikipedia, forms New England's largest estuary. We were drawn to the Newport Folk Music Festival. It featured headliners Joan Baez, Bob Dylan, Pete Seeger, Peter, Paul & Mary, et *al.*, old-timers such as Lightnin' Hopkins, and young blood. Morgan did not join us in Newport.

In Newport, we camped in tents in the backyard of relatives of one of the summer students. So, I saved on lodging, and I could have *really* done the trip on the cheap, except that I had to eat. My Maryland summer, following up on my Bensonhurst/Sunset summer job, occasioned at least a second time when my shortage of pocket cash got me in a bind. (To reiterate, all my paychecks were endorsed and signed over to Stepdad—my solemn duty to help pay for my education. And the "trickle down" was often just that.) When our laboratory vans made stops at a Howard Johnson or roadside eatery, I just stayed behind, until one of the faculty members noticed. He upbraided me: "You are not supposed to starve yourself!" I don't recall if he lent me the money, or whether he treated me on personal/lab funds, but I did not have to go on a hunger strike on that trip.

Back to Morgan—I could not believe my good fortune. Her dad was an offbeat artist type with dealings of some sort with the federal government. He was tall, loose, and lanky, with a rakish full mustache and a jaunty way about him, as if about to spring a punchline. In my view, Dad was great. Hey, we were guys, and that went a long way. Once, during a lovely garden lunch at her home, Morgan spilled a salad on her lap. Dad called the play-by-play, "There is oil and vinegar on your lap, lettuce on your thighs, and a cherry tomato on your cherry." Morgan, a fine Southern lady, was duly mortified.

On another occasion, I was hard on the hunt for a lovely butterfly at Morgan's home. She felt ignored, and enticingly flitted and fluttered like a rare fritillary. I obliged by trying to net her, gently. Dad caught the action and smirked and even gave a semi-approving chuckle. Later he told me, "I like you. I know you're a gentleman. Morgan is precious to me as she is to you." Enough said. I understood.

Calvert County, site of the Solomons Lab and named after the English founders of Maryland, was officially in southern Maryland, though I recall a road sign claiming, "Welcome to South Southern Maryland." The Mason-Dixon line separated Pennsylvania (and Delaware) from Maryland, and the distance south of the Pennsylvania border was proportional to "Southern character." I saw an example of this character: A very nice Black lady cleaned the lab weekly, assisted by her two well-behaved adolescent boys. Dr. Joe told me that Mom shot her husband dead when she caught him *in flagrante delicto* with another woman. She was let off, apparently for a justifiable crime of passion. So, in the South, look over your shoulder for a scorned woman, or a miffed boyfriend.

BROOKLYN 1956

From: Stuyvesant classmate, Arty Aptowitz, Personnel Director for the Office of the Brooklyn Borough President, 1978-1988
(05/16/2001)

I search for coins fallen from the laundry strung upside-
down on lines run to telephone poles
Pennies, nickels, dimes, the Holy Grail quarter
Feed my need for Hershey Bars and balsa airplanes
  that I fly like Berra's ball slicing toward the chalk line
  'til snatched by Amoros

Brooklyn, not Spike Lee's Crooklyn
There's no "them"
Just me and my friends
And a pink Spauldeen bounding ever-upward

From my window on the hill rising from the Parkway
I can see Coney Island and Rockaway too
Fireworks from one on Tuesday, the other on Wednesday
Illuminate my southern sky

I know the cracks on the sidewalk like the lines on my
  hand
I could go back now to that apartment on the hill
Step the parquet floor and caress the molded wall
Brooklyn—The last exit on the Lexington Express is home

PART II

A Man-Child Beyond

(1966 to 1990)

I made it out of Bensonhurst and Brooklyn but had to travel further to break the bonds of boyhood.

Candid shot (1968) in the lab of Samson R. Gross, Duke Biochemistry Dept. No, that is not a beer cooler, but a cold box with instrumentation to separate proteins. (In this case, it held chromatography columns and a fraction collector.) Amazing to me that I had hair back then, and black. Ringless left hand tells me this was before Mary and I married (Dec 31, 1968).

Dr. Gross was the paparazzo.

Chapter Fifteen

. . .

DURHAM: RETURN TO DIXIE
(1966–1971)

> Do we need to tread the same road twice
> To relearn trail marks along the way?
> And face and pay the same toll price?
> Lessons relearned can our doubts allay

I look back at my post-baccalaureate years and ask if grad school really marked an entry into "manhood." The case for it is buttressed by marriage, fatherhood, and enhanced awareness of racial injustice. But, sometimes I'm a real *stunad*. My summer 1964 hikes to and from Miami should have filled my Dixie cup. But I was *meshuggeneh in (Dixie) kop*—crazy in the head, my hard head/*capo dosto* that runneth over.

Yes, I chose Durham, North Carolina, home of Duke University, to pursue a PhD. And did my cup overflow—to the extent that I mark this choice as my first, though initially furtive, step to manhood.

Joe, pray tell why you made such a choice? Was my summer in "South Southern Maryland" a reentry portal to the South? Or did I somehow equate Durham, NC and Ithaca, NY? Certainly, Dookies liked to call their university "the Harvard of the South." Duke's basketball team wasn't so bad, and a cool young lady (not Morgan) I met in Maryland was studying there.

All those considerations aside, the *real* reason I chose Duke was their graduate catalog. I pulled it off a shelf at Cornell's Uris Library, the one with the bell tower and chimes. The catalog spoke to me; bells rang. Really.

I applied to Duke, and they had the nerve to put me on a waiting list. Soon after, I received an offer *cum* research stipend. I accepted to let them know what they almost passed up. This was the cocky side of my split personality, between man and child.

I threw myself at Duke, even though I had never visited my southern suitor. This was now becoming a pattern—four years earlier I got on a Greyhound bus in New York City's Port Authority to travel up to Ithaca for the first time, to the arms of my alma mater, Cornell U. I was an academic war bride. This time I *flew* to Raleigh-Durham Airport, a step up.

I caught the airport shuttle to Durham and was the last passenger in the van when the driver asked my destination. (Not sure he called me "boy" or "son," but I felt stripped of any pretense at sophistication. Southerners had a way of letting you know your social level.) I suggested a motel near Duke, one not too expensive. The rates indeed were reasonable, and the desk clerk in the one-story humble brick structure was a kindly old man.

"Where can I find a pay phone?" I asked, forgetting to address him as "sir." (And also forgetting that I could probably use the room phone.)

"Why, there's one just outside the lobby." His florid accent blew me away, making me wonder if my Bensonhurst brogue grated on him.

The booth was to be the scene of a crime against Ma Bell. My other mother and I had a plot: I call collect, identifying myself as "Lou D'Agostino," my stepfather's name, and ask to speak with Joe Polacco. This signals to Mamma that I arrived safely, so she follows with "I'm sorry, he isn't home." The problem with this theater was the operator. No way could I get through to her, though *Polacco* and *D'Agostino* were perfectly normal last names—in Bensonhurst.

"Suh, I cain't understayand you!!"

"I want to make a collect call to Joe Polacco from Lou D'Agostino." Yes, I was speaking a foreign language, my accent accentuated by my guilt at trying to bilk Ma Bell.

Finally, the operator relayed an unintelligible request, and somehow Mamma knew I was OK. Oh, I would someday pay for the ruse. You don't have to be Catholic or Jewish or a Jehovah's Witness, to be cast under Guilt's long shadow.

On my way back to the lobby, a young Black man asked if I could give him a lift to Haiti (pronounced Hay-TIE, which I soon learned was Hayti). I had no idea, and no car (and still no driver's license). He was exasperated at my confusion, so he clarified "N----- Town!" Welcome to the South, yet again, Joe.

The next day my Duke entry was equally inauspicious. Eight-plus weeks in Chiquila, Honduras, an arduous journey through Mexico, and a stint in Las Vegas did not constitute a summer immersed in biochemical concepts and experimental design. Dr. Irwin Fridovich, head of graduate studies in biochemistry, was extremely gracious in the face of my atrocious entrance exam scores. In his lovely (and oh so comforting) New York City accent, he praised my altruistic summer ("laudable") and added that no one did well in physical chemistry. Chastened, I knew I needed to live a more academic lifestyle, though not monastic, for I did engage in intramurals, spelunking, the rugby club, etc. (All work and no play . . .)

On the way to my "man phase," I did take two juvenile off-ramps.

Off-ramp 1. We first-year grad students were obliged to take medical biochemistry, which we called "Baby Biochem." Most taking the course were first-year medical students. We interacted with them like oil with water. The med students complained about the demands of the course, and even had the audacity to call it "Chem." Philip Handler was our renowned biochemistry chair (who, in 1969 became head of the National Academy of Science) and taught many of the lectures. Dr. Handler lent a willing ear to the med students' complaints, even during lectures.

The med students were obviously in awe. Dr. Handler had flair: "I don't know anything about photosynthesis, but I'll tell you what I do know," was his preamble to a fireside chat armed with just a fat piece of chalk and the blackboard.

About three-quarters into a lecture, Dr. Handler would look out across the audience, put his foot on a stool, and light up a cigarette as he was about to make an important point, *the* point. (I do not think indoor smoking was prohibited in North Carolina, and, hey, this was Duke, founded by tobacco money.) I was part of a cabal of three or four male grad students, and we made a pact to light up cigars at Handler's next "Humphry Bogart moment." We lit up, my heart pounding. Handler looked very disturbed but said nothing. A young lady medical student left the lecture hall, apparently sickened by the cigar smoke, at least that was what I was later told.

Off-ramp 2. Baby Biochem was in fall semester. Come spring, we were feeling frisky and emulated the builders of Stonehenge by moving a very sizeable boulder into the research building, to block entry into the lab of a faculty member who was making our life miserable in his biochemical techniques course. (He took the prank in good spirits, posing in his lab coat with his foot on the huge rock, mason's hammer in hand.)

I point out these two incidents to show that I had not been fully *bar mitzvahed* over my first year of graduate school, the first year of "my adulthood," of being an official *mentsh*. Yes, Salvatore, I was still very much a Bensonhurst boy.

Happily, I justified Duke's faith in me: Two years into my stay I put in an all-star performance on the doctoral comprehensive exams. Over five-plus years, Duke was an exciting, intellectually invigorating, scientific experience.

Duke and Cornell had parallels. Cornell was the youngest Ivy League school, established in 1865, but Duke was even farther from a venerable antebellum vestige of Southern culture. Its main (West) campus was an academic Disney Land, built up almost overnight in the 1930s in the piney woods (later "Duke Forest") of the North Carolina Piedmont. West Campus was instant gothic, including a Methodist/ecumenical chapel that looked to me more like a cathedral. The campus and chapel were financed by Duke family tobacco money and built by an unusually high concentration of imported Italian stone masons. I had *that* connection, at least.

The East Campus, of Georgian architecture and much older vintage, was incorporated into the greater Duke University. Women lived on East Campus, though they attended coeducational classes on West Campus, 1.8 miles away, accessible by shuttle bus—for them in the early days, *only* by bus.

I rented a room in a boardinghouse between East and West Campus, just off the shuttle bus run. My sixtyish, redheaded landlady at times seemed a Southern version of the *Arsenic and Old Lace* landlady, but I did not fear for my safety, almost never. One evening, perhaps a little inebriated, she knocked on my door expressing concern at the "arguing" voices coming out of a neighboring room, rented to two Korean students. I was able to calm her then, and we got along just fine in general. When, a year later, we said our goodbyes, she sent me off with a smiling, "You're a fine-looking young man!" Compliments and insults tend to have long half-lives though the compliments tend more to find refuge in this retrospective.

While the shuttle bus was a way to meet women, my first year was a couple of steps down from social life at Cornell. Many women seemed to embody "Southern Belle" attitudes, and I had trouble playing "Beauregard." (Oh, did I mention that Morgan "Dear Johned" me late in my Cornell senior year?) Social contacts for a graduate student were limited. I was no longer known for athletics or campus involvement, though Duke rugby helped. Whereas Cornell was a center of activism, Duke seemed to try to maintain itself as a southern island of academia and charm.

But on campus and within and outside Durham, America was undergoing racial and social upheaval, and I got caught up in it. Just a sampling: riots/rebellions in Watts (1965), Detroit (1967), and Newark (1967), a massacre of protesting Black college students at Orangeburg (SC) State (February 1968) barely two months before the assassination of Martin Luther King. Vietnam was a gaping wound—we grad students were eligible for the draft.

However, through all this my rough edges were "rounded," my speech slowed down, and I could even engage in small talk. I learned to appreciate and compare styles of barbecue and hush puppies. I was involved in summer softball, fall intramurals, and the excellent Duke rugby club. Durham was still in transition from a Southern "company town" (tobacco) or "mill town" (textiles) to more of a college town, though not Ivy League, not even the Chapel Hill of our rival University of North Carolina.

Durham offered bars and clubs, and most a little dangerous. The Stallion Club, just outside town, was as large as an airplane hangar and served Black clientele. Oft-times fellow graduate student, Mary Schaeffer, and I were the only white folks there. (By this time, I had a driver's license and a car, and Mary and I were definitely "steadies.") As in all clubs, bars, and restaurants, we learned to live with the bizarre North Carolina custom of "setups." Liquor-by-the-drink was illegal, but one could enter an establishment with a bottle of hootch—bought at a state-controlled liquor store—and keep it in a brown bag under the table. We ordered setups and poured booze into cups of ice and mixers. At the Stallion Club, serious-looking uniformed Brothers, with nightsticks, made the rounds to make sure the booze was under the table, in proper brown bags. The "Brown Bagging" song made the rounds on the radio, but at the Stallion the music was live and the dancing fantastic—and so tough to stay current with Watusi, locomotion, mashed potatoes, African twist, funky chicken, and anything by James Brown. The late '60s were the apogee of soul music (Sam Cooke, Aretha Franklin, Marvin Gaye, et *al.*)

I worked in the laboratory of Samson R Gross, a nice Jewish boy from, of all places, Bensonhurst. (His wife was Orthodox—from Williamsburg—Brooklyn, that is.) Dr. Gross was an excellent geneticist. Though we usually had a tumultuous relationship, I greatly benefited from his expertise, and we loved exchanging Bensonhurst stories. We agreed that Sicilian-Neapolitan was akin to the Litvak-Galitzianer divide among the Ashkenazim—if you were from Bensonhurst, or from Brooklyn in general, no further explanation needed. Over the sabbatical year that Dr. Gross spent in the Weizmann Institute of Science in Tel Aviv, I grew up as an independent scientist, although he might not have fully agreed with that assessment.

I also grew up in responsibility. Mary Schaeffer and I married. We first met while measuring mitochondrial respiration with a Warburg manometer—an apparatus that brings tears to the eyes of biochemistry history buffs. In our small first-year class of ca. ten biochemistry students, I had daily contact with Mary. When we married, my life was radically changed, for the better, and when our Laura was born about a year later, my life was blessed.

Duke was more than an educational and scientific training ground. It was a window into racially divided America. In its research labs, students were generally white, and lab personnel Black. Our chief lab technician, Evelyn G, was a competent and dignified lady whose husband was the chauffer of Duke's president. Robbie G was a feisty young lady tech with whom I developed a close relationship. Slowly, the realization came out that her boyfriend was killed by the police. I never learned the circumstances, and I never asked. She did tell me in a moment of confidence that he "passed away."

Robbie let on that Evelyn was able to get into a "lighter skin" sorority, though to me Evelyn was a fighter for racial justice. I was at Evelyn's place when her daughter yelled excitedly that Andrew Young was running for US Representative from Georgia. When

Evelyn retired from her tech job, there was a lab celebration in which I read her a poetic ode ("Big Ev"), a take-off on the lyrics to Jimmy Dean's "Big Bad John." I have lost and forgotten the lyrics, but they earned me a great big hug, which I have not forgotten. ("Every day at the lab, you can see her arrive. She runs the show and takes no jive . . ." Lines to that effect, lines indeed best forgotten.)

For off-campus parties, however, Robbie's apartment was *the* place. Mary and I were usually the only white couple. One night, I got into an intense discussion with one of Robbie's buddies from Durham's North Carolina Central College (a 1909 HBCU institution, now NC Central University). It was indeed a discussion, an exchange of points of view, and entirely civil, but instilled in me the intensity of racial feeling just under the skin.

For me, Duke became more "interesting" than Cornell, even if Cornell had a seventy-year head start. The assassination of Dr. Martin Luther King radicalized me, to the extent I could be radicalized. Mary and I took part in a campus sit-in and voter registration drives in Black Durham. ("You be careful, son" was an admonition I frequently got from Black folks.) I did some tutoring/mentorship of a Black youngster until his grandma put a stop to it. Fellow grad students and I went to Fort Bragg on Armed Forces Day to protest the war, hear (check) out Jane Fonda, and catch glimpses of the Chicago Seven. Vietnam seemed to be a war borne on the backs of many Blacks, and Muhammed Ali's "I ain't got no quarrel with them Viet Cong" still resonates.

On campus, I attended events by Harlem Congressman Adam Clayton Powell (complete with a phoned-in bomb threat), comedian-activist Dick Gregory, and James Brown (in concert). I witnessed a confederate flag burning in the stands at a football game, and a sixty-something Dixie patriot physically confronting the Black students who easily outnumbered him. Black Power fists were raised and boos arose from the crowd, but I was not sure of the targets.

Between the lab personnel and activities in town, it seemed to me that Durham was at least 50 percent Black. It certainly hosted the largest Black-owned business in the US—North Carolina Mutual Life Insurance—also the name of Durham's tallest building, and a target of racist verbal sniping ("a monument to damn n——s").

Oh, I saw that racism up close. Two fellow students and I (still single) found a great rental, a house with a well-appointed kitchen, three bedrooms, spacious living room, one and a half baths, a backyard garden, and a long driveway off a secondary highway. It was less than five miles from campus in the quiet countryside. The home of the landlord was on the other side of the driveway. He was a personable fellow named JD, and I would not be surprised if JD stood for Jefferson Davis. (His last name is excised from this account.) JD had a strong accent and spoke very fast, while inhaling and exhaling so as not to waste his life force. He was bald, a bull of a man with a prosperous paunch, so appropriate for Bull Durham, the tobacco that made Durham famous—indeed, JD's expansive front lawn smelled of tobacco powder, a local fertilizer swept from the floors of Durham's tobacco and cigarette factories.

We three grad students pieced together how that rental became available: JD's wife owned Sally's Beauty Parlor, housed in what later became our living room/kitchen/half-bath. Sally refused to serve Black ladies, and lawyer Floyd McKissick represented the denied. When Sally lost the case, the parlor was closed, remodeled, and three bedrooms and a full bath were appended. It became a rental. (One of my roommates prominently displayed a retrieved Sally's Beauty Parlor sign in his bedroom.)

Once, when I was over on JD's side to leave off a rent payment, his TV showed Mr. McKissick being interviewed on a separate issue.

JD commented to me, "Now that is one sorry n——. Don't you have any n——s at your place. I'll kick y'all outta here."

This brought a recollection of Robbie's response when I invited her over. "Yeah, Joe, in the dark of night."

(That "sorry" Mr. McKissick later founded Soul City in a very poor NC county. It was successful for a few years before facing insurmountable financial problems.)

To JD, my Mediterranean roots were passable. I was in a sufficiently light zone of the pigment gradient.

"I like you, Joe. You remind me of Tony Canzoneri. Heh heh heh."

Tony was a tough boxer. In 1967, he was fifty-nine years old, but I knew of him as an Italian American legend—a rarity as a three-weight division world boxing champion.

JD's love for folks of Mediterranean descent included Greek Americans. He was a supporter of Nick Galifianakis (immigrant son, ex-marine, and Duke professor), who represented Durham's district in Congress over three consecutive terms, 1967–1973, during the waning days of the Solid Democratic South. In his 1972 campaign to step up to the US Senate, Nick was defeated by Republican Jesse Helms (of the mantra "he's one of us").

I lived those times and there is no need for retroactive racial enlightenment—if I did not stand up to JD then, I cannot crow now. In fall 1967, JD railed against the marriage of the only daughter of Dean Rusk (secretary of state under JFK and LBJ) to a "Negro," as so identified in a *NY Times* frontpage article

(September 22, 1967). JD went on about the televised shame of Rusk walking his daughter down the aisle, and how miscegenation was "mongrelizing" the white race. I shared the guilt by saying nothing, and I certainly thought better than to defend the marriage with genetic arguments of "hybrid vigor" and "heterosis."

Yet, JD's racism also showed a surprisingly human side. His personal "boy," that "N—— Red," lived on JD's extensive wooded property. Red drowned in a swimming hole on that property, and JD was devastated.

"That damned fool went and got himself drowned."

"Sorry to hear that, JD. I read about it in the papers," I said. I did not know Red was JD's "boy."

JD looked into my eyes with sincere sorrow. "He was just a slave!!"

Relationships are always complex, and with JD there were also humorous moments, more associated with clashes of culture than of race. I gifted Sally and JD a wedge of well-aged, sharp, oily, and aromatic provolone cheese I had picked up on a trip to a Bensonhurst *Salumeria e Latticini* (salami and cheese store). Sally thanked me at her door, and as I turned to wave goodbye, she was sniffing the cheese and looking at me with complete lack of belief, bereft of trust or pleasure.

This was one unsuccessful intrusion of Sal La Puma's Bensonhurst into Sally's Carolina Piedmont.

I got the upshot later from JD:

"Thank you, Joe! Hooh boy, that cheese was RANK! I mean they musta tried to milk the bull, heh heh heh. But it was very good of you. We really appreciate it."

"Don't think anything of it, JD," I said, fighting images of the cheese feeding blessed vermin in a landfill.

My stay with JD ended when I moved out to Mary Schaeffer's apartment in town. Soon after, we were engaged. My ex-roommates at "Rancho JD" were eventually evicted for entertaining people of color. I did not miss JD. A memory of him is his smiling at me one day and saying something like, "Joe, you kill me (in a manner of speaking). I'm getting my rifle and I'll shoot you up and down and split you in two." He said this while picking and eating apricots from one of his trees. I am sorry to say that he evoked images of a pot-bellied orangutan.

Bensonhurst invades Durham. Becoming a father started my earnest transition to adulthood. Mary and I married New Year's Eve 1968, and she presented me with a daughter shortly after New Year's Day (1970; count the months). Mamma Vina flew down from New York soon after. The plane skidded in a rare snowstorm while landing in Raleigh-Durham. The pilot announced that they slipped off the runway and that a bus would retrieve the passengers to take them to the terminal. Upon hearing this, Mamma "sort of" yelled, "Well, he should have used snow tires!" The accent and the spontaneity raised nervous laughter. Inside the terminal, Mamma gave a sweet hello to a young Black lady.

"Joseph, when the plane skidded, she was making the sign of the cross. I asked her if she was scared, and she nodded, yes." So, Mamma bonded with a North Carolinian even before the plane unloaded. Bensonhurst strikes again.

Naturally, Mamma went absolutely nuts over baby Laura, her first grandchild. (I'm related to my mother. An attending nurse told Mary that she never saw a new father go so nuts.) To me, the bigger story was how Mamma was so natural overall in a very foreign environment. And people loved her, even as this

Bensonhurst émigré went down the bread aisle of Piggly Wiggly, squeezing every loaf and yelling, "Joseph, they're all sponges!!"

So, our daily loaves were out, but there was still fish. Mary and I usually bought our seafood in a local Durham shop. (Piggly Wiggly and seafood were not an appetizing duet.) The shop's proprietor was a dead ringer for nervous Barney Fife (Don Knotts), the assistant to Sheriff Andy Taylor (Andy Griffith) of TV's "Mayberry, NC." Our local Barney had a raucous and loud pet macaw that evinced frequent cries of "HU-USH, John!" from his owner. Mamma picked up on this and perfected the accent, parroting it throughout her stay.

Oh, so, Mr. Knotts, you don't have squid or octopus. We'll buy your frozen squid *bait*. Mamma turned those frigid eight-inch cubes to a component of *linguine ai frutti di mare*—heavenly.

But the twain did meet more directly between the South of Italy and the American South where black-eyed peas and greens (collards, for example) were staples. Poverty was the common factor. For us *paesani* of the *Mezzogiorno*, beans and greens were components of survival food that went almost *haute cuisine* in the New World: *pasta e fagioli* and *broccoli di rapa* (beans and macaroni, and broccoli "robbies"), for instance—cheap and nourishing. So, Mamma had raw material for some real Italian soul food.

Pizza was becoming an American soul food, and Batman (Bartolomeo) was a proselytizer, a missionary. Batman did not descend from Duke's imported Italian stone masons; he came from a family stopover in New Jersey. From there he and his wife took their daughter to Duke Hospital, and she was "saved" from an affliction that I do not recall. Mr. and Mrs. Bat stayed in town and opened a successful pizzeria. I loved speaking New Jersey dialect with him. Bat entertained the clientele while his wife labored in the kitchen.

"Hey, Batman, don't you feel guilty that you're schmoozing with the customers up front while the missus is cooking and cleaning in back?"

"Nah, I make it up to her. At night I go to bed in my baby doll pajamas. All is good," to which Mrs. Bat gave a believable laughing endorsement.

Mamma Vina wasn't so sure she liked Bat, but she acknowledged he was a showman.

To me, Durham transformed itself from a cultural wasteland to a rich and varied experience. I close out with mention of two special people (among several), Miss Patty K. and Dr. Carlos Corredor.

Miss Patty K. She washed lab glassware and kept our lab clean and functional. Robbie always greeted her as "Good Morning/Hello/How are you? Miss Patty." She was a sweet lady, to me middle-aged, and we hit it off. I did not know the racial affronts she endured. Patty lost a daughter well before I joined the lab, and I was never privy to the circumstances. Patty had legal representation, and one day she came back from a court date extremely upset. She did not want to talk about it, and we never did.

I made her laugh in other situations. She loved that Mary and I "kept" our infant daughter, Laura, in an empty office in a hospital-issued "baby box." (Mary would come down from her upstairs lab to breastfeed Laura.) Patty and Evelyn checked in on Laura quite often.

I think both Patty and Evelyn developed maternal feelings for Mary and me. When I left the Gross lab, Patty gave me a present with a card saying, "Gonna miss you." I still get emotional reliving that moment. At the time, I could only thank her profusely.

Carlos Corredor. Carlos was upgrading his biochemistry degree to a PhD at Duke, thence to return to his faculty position at the Universidad del Valle in Cali, Colombia. He invited Mary and me to visit Cali—they were hiring faculty in a Rockefeller Foundation-funded program to upgrade the scientific training of Colombian professors (who hailed from universities throughout their country).

Carlos returned to Colombia with his PhD, and we had agreed to visit him there. I got cold feet about moving to Cali to set up our research programs, but when Mary saw Carlos' postcards and other Cali propaganda, her response was, "Let's go." It wasn't, "Let's check it out," it was "Let's go!" Soon after receiving our PhDs, we moved to Cali, Colombia, after packing our appliances while dealing with Mary's morning sickness. Luckily, we did not need a visa for Joseph Michael Polacco (b. July 25, 1972, Cali, Colombia).

Goodbye, Durham, rife with memories and experiences:

- The segregated courthouse in East Carolina—no signs, people just knew. We white college kids from Durham found ourselves on "the wrong side" of the audience for this traffic case.

- The downtown Durham diner that would not serve me a "bo-burger" because it sounded indecent. (It was a traditional Ithaca, New York cheeseburger adorned with a fried egg.)

- Arthur and Laura Olshan, our Jewish counterparts from Far Rockaway, Queens—great companions and fellow parents of a young daughter.

And so much more. Might you imagine the setting of the next chapter of my developing manhood?

It almost didn't happen. The US Army made a call.

66 *Bob Smith from Brooklyn is a guy who sometimes gets hung with problems and fears. Wolfman Jack is a happy-go-lucky guy who knows how to party. The challenge of my life has been letting more and more of Bob Smith go, becoming the Wolfman on an almost full-time basis, while still taking care of business.* 99

—Wolfman Jack

Chapter Sixteen

• • •

REGISTRATION

Duke (1966) and Military (1971)

> We are fodder for the political elite
> To whom we must prove we're not effete
> While we're pulled in opposing directions
> We've little time to make valid reflections

Before Mary and I could move to Colombia (Feb. 1972), and before baby Joseph was born (July 1972), the US Army made a call. And, the timing was due to a hasty item I put down on an academic registration form at Duke in September 1966.

Please bear with this flashback: Duke graduate school registration was more "computerized" and streamlined than was Cornell's, four years before. We filled out computer cards that featured inscrutably arranged upright rectangular window openings. One card's written code in the lower right corner was perplexing, "SS-34," I recall. I did not dwell much on it, SS making me think of Storm Troopers, or perhaps the SS Duke Academia, the dreadnought taking me to a PhD. There was an easy question on the card: "Expected date of graduation." I simply projected four years, less three months, or June 1970—a twofold mistake. It takes more than eight semesters to "get" a PhD (you *become* one), and a potentially fatal mistake: I was draft age, and when I was finished with school, I would be draft eligible. The SS stood for "Selective Service." (The "34" may have come from my muddled memory of the SS34 centrifuge rotor I used almost every day in my doctoral research.)

I should have put more thought into that date: Over my last two years at Cornell, my classmates and I took note of how many GIs died each week in Vietnam. It was the "body count" era; we always got more of them than they got of us. We were winning.

Yippie.

The summer before my junior year (Honduras, 1964) I learned of the Gulf of Tonkin "incident." As I mentioned in Chapter Thirteen my initial response was to go there and "kick butt." In time, we learned of our government's duplicity in that attack.

The U. S. goal was "containment." In that summer 1964, the Alliance for Progress was quite viable, and there were Peace Corps volunteers all over Honduras. One unspoken goal of each program—perhaps *the* goal—was to counter Castroism. We wanted to stop those dominoes from falling not only in Southeast Asia, but also in Latin America.

Now, spring forward to late spring 1971: Mary and I were married, parents of eighteen-month-old Laura, and we were trying to finish our doctoral dissertations to get on with our careers. (Mary had taken time off to have Laura then changed her dissertation research upon her return [because she had been "scooped"], and still finished before me.)

As a graduate student, I had a deferment, and then I didn't. When the deferment ended, we were dealing with draft lotteries, and my number was high—no way they would get to me. And then they did. In spring 1971, I got a notice to appear for a preinduction physical at a facility in Raleigh, North Carolina, some thirty miles away. I was the oldest passenger on a bus of Dookie undergrads. The atmosphere was that of a class trip to the Museum of Natural History or the Bronx Zoo. Most kids were certain they had an "out" while a few actually *wanted* to go to 'nam.

We were herded into a classroom to take an aptitude test, and I felt like I did during my grad school first-year achievement exams. Apparently, I had the right stuff, though many undergrads kicked my butt. On the exam's first page, we were asked to enter a code for our level of formal education. The military had a mysterious system for encoding years completed in high school or college. I raised my hand asking the code for *fifth-year graduate student*. The MC looked equal parts annoyed and befuddled. He left the room and came back with a short letter-number combo. I don't recall if they distinguished upper and lower case, but I felt like an undistinguished nonmilitary case.

The physical was definitely an assembly line. For instance, we all dropped our BVDs, bent over, and spread our cheeks so the proper medical official could walk the line to confirm that all was A(nal)-OK.

On the bus, I had learned of a high blood pressure tactic: Spend two or more weeks on an exclusive Chianti and Cheddar cheese diet. I heard a probably apocryphal story that the doc in one case sent a kid directly to a cardiac ward, so high was his blood pressure.

There were other ploys. Mine was my football knee.

I carried a letter from Doc Rachun at Cornell football/student health, explaining the trauma (including torn cartilage) my left knee suffered. He was as literary and supportive as he could be. The reader's face danced between exasperation and contempt. In contrast, a Duke football player with a *really* bad knee pleaded for a 1A status.

The letter got me a ticket to Fort Bragg to see a specialist. The bus ticket was a tapeworm of small towns, and at each I ripped off the last ticket segment to change to a bus to the next town. I finally landed in Fayetteville and shared a taxi to the base with a uniformed much older guy who asked if I were a veteran. I explained that I was a Duke graduate student with no military experience.

Fort Bragg was even more of a meat-processing plant, but I finally got to see a specialist who appeared to be on my side, prodding me to express pain as he manhandled and manipulated my knee. His long write-up was in my hand as I reported to another line, again in my BVDs. I was able to read through his handwritten medical terminology, but the final sentence was all I needed: "Patient is fit for induction."

I was met by Mary and baby Laura at the Durham bus depot and was energized to action. I wrote a letter to my draft board, explaining the investment Mary and I had made in our doctoral programs and in building our (growing) family, and how military service would be very disruptive, and indeed vitiating Uncle Sam's investments in our fellowships (under the National Defense and Education Act). I don't think I used the word "vitiate."

Before I married, one of my roommates at JD's place was a likeable fellow from South Carolina. He was in a PhD program, in physiology I think, and was classified 1A. He just up and declared that if called, he would serve. I do not know what became of him.

I would not go softly into that night.

I followed up my letter with a personal visit to my draft board (in Coney Island), experiencing love at first sight with the first person I came upon. She was a matriarchal Jewish lady with a strong Brooklyn accent. (Italians and Jews have their own subtly different Brooklyn accents—if subtlety can be a descriptor of our native tongue.) I knew I was in good hands, and so glad the board was not in South Carolina. A few weeks later—I got notice that I was given a "family deferment."

If I had been drafted, what would I have done? From this long perspective it's hard to say. Seeking refuge in Canada was an option, and I knew several who took it. I know for certain, though, that if I found myself in a Vietnamese jungle, under the leadership of a second lieutenant, though I resented the wise guy, I probably would have done something stupid under his command, like leading a charge or running reconnaissance. I'm not brave, but incredibly pliant (a *shnook*, a *chooch*). Even if I survived, I could have developed a drug addiction—that was one affliction I avoided my whole life.

Thank you, my Jewish mother on the Coney Island draft board.

A word about the draft: I hated it, of course, but I wish it were back. The draft behooved us, the eligible, to investigate whether a military action was legitimate, not a wheel in some political or economic vehicle, the drivers *feeding a hunger cadaverous* (Chapter Six).

Without the draft, we'd have been in 'nam with a volunteer army, with the rest of us "thankful for their service." Reading about battles won and lost is now almost like looking at results on the sports page. Today, some of us deride immigration across our southern border, but fellow citizens, look at the rosters of our combat soldiers—the list has a definite Latino flavor, *cierto?*

The draft was not an issue in Bensonhurst during World War II. Most of the young Sicilian studs couldn't wait to kill Nazis and Japs, though Frankie Primo confessed to his secret paramour, Sylvia Cohen, that he wasn't sure he could kill anybody, even Nazis. He told Sylvia that moms cried but they wanted "their sons to go. It's patriotic. *We have to show we don't side with Italy.*" (My italics: *The Boys of Bensonhurst [1942].*)

Chapter Seventeen

...

BEAUTIFUL ETHEREAL HUILA
(Cali, Colombia, 1972)

Ethereal Huila, glacial above our travails
Do you bide time to your violent rebirth?
While we busy ants, scurry mountain trails
Under your floating fury, extolling our worth

Oh, Placid Lady in white-laced shawls
Will you mete upon us violent destiny
As we strut within your stone firewalls?
Oh please, forbear our impish tenancy!

Mary and I lived two years in Cali, Colombia, returning to the US in late 1973. Since my return, I certainly have not ignored Colombia's "War on Drugs," the FARC, paramilitaries, drug cartels, Pablo Escobar, and Cali's world-class salsa—the dance, that is.

But now I am tuned into Cali more than ever.

Why?

Perhaps my retirement from academia and my broader world perspective have returned me to that treacherous, enchanting, endearing, enraging place: "*Cali, sucursal del cielo*—Cali, a branch of heaven." When I left Cali, indeed for the very reasons I left it, I was immediately thrust into the American "fast lanes" of career and family. I focused on what was ahead and strove to keep pace. Back in Cali, however, I often doubted my goals and place in the world at large. In truth, I knew the world resembled Cali more than it resembled America. It was easier to shut out that realization when I returned to America and rapidly reengaged my wheels on the academic tracks of competitive science.

The mellow years of retirement have reoriented those tracks, which now veer back to those tumultuous, frustrating, yet contemplative years in Latin America.

Universidad del Valle, Cali, Colombia, 1972. Mary and I were brand new PhDs. We were warmly welcomed by our Universidad del Valle colleagues in a well-funded program to improve the level of biomedical research and teaching in Colombia. As mentioned on page 144, we were involved in advancing the academic degrees of science professors from universities throughout Colombia. And, we taught local undergrads and medical students.

In Cali, I saw stark contrasts everywhere and I often wondered at the sincerity of our effusive and warm reception. "Doctor, we are *muy agradecidos* (very thankful) that you are here; we look forward to working with you and learning from you. (*Yeah, RIGHT, you're filling a position better taken by a colombiano, and after two or three years you will escape back to your gringo paradise.*)

Students clamored to work under our direction, but were they exploiting *us* while they held their collective nose?

We received funding from the Rockefeller Foundation, and that name was a catch-all for *yanqui* imperialism, even genocide (sterilization), under the guise of research. We arrived on campus on the first anniversary of a student slaying by the army in Bogotá. The Cali campus was embroiled in protest, and eventually the army came in, putting us under Marshall Law. One morning, I joined my colleagues in the relative safety of a rooftop perch, looking down on students in pitched battles with the military.

And looking out, in the distance, I spied her—beautiful, floating above the clouds, almost a snow white fairy, *una hada blanca.*

"What's that?" I asked my colleagues.

"The Huila Glacier" came to me, almost as a chorus of response.

"¡O qué lindo!" I answered, momentarily lost to the danger gathering below us. Huila with its white shawl appeared to put its placid benediction on the *locura*, the craziness at its feet. I learned much later that there was craziness in the very bowels of the Goddess Huila. She could release the bound magma fury of tectonic plate subduction.

Students were entering our building. At the roof railing, a colleague at my elbow, a spirited, young, Colombian lady, turned to me:

"And now they come for the gringos."

Was she 100 percent kidding? She and I danced a cumbia or two only a week before at one of Cali's many social gatherings.

The *real* dizzying feature of our rooftop encounter was that only months before, I was a student protestor at Duke, but now identified as a lackey of the imperialist class in Cali.

At the building's entrance, things seemed to quiet a little. Our group of faculty, technicians, and staff tentatively walked downstairs. On the stairs, students were marching to the fifth and top floor, my floor. The metallic stairwell reverberated to the synchronized student chants, almost as if we were experiencing another of our too-frequent earthquakes: *"Down* with bourgeois exploitation of students! *"¡¡ABAJO!!"* was the chorus. *"Down* with yanqui imperialism!" *"¡¡ABAJO!!"*

I came eye-to-eye with a baseball teammate. He greeted me with a *"Hola, Profesor."* On the diamond I was "José" or simply, "Polacco." This fragmentation of formality and feelings—a miasma of multicolored confetti—was dizzying, disorienting. Was I engaged in research aimed at genocide, or was I training Colombia's new scientists? Was I "acculturating" to communicate science in my new environment? Or was I merely enjoying the best of tropical variety, the addictive throbbing of Latino delights?

Or did I really care?

Now I know the answer.

I fiercely cared, and still do. From Honduras to Colombia, I am plugged into the challenges facing our Latin American *hermanos* (brothers and sisters).

While I hope that Huila's roiling volcanic interior holds off for a couple more centuries, there are more urgent human cataclysms to address.

Huila Glacier seen from a higher altitude. From my roof vantage point in Cali, it was floating on the clouds—a snow pyramid on a blue background.

Our ragtag team, after a notable victory. While we did not sport many stars, we did indeed have personalities (other than Bensonhurst Joe, #12). To my left Fernando, nephew of Omar Torrijos, Panamanian strongman who signed the 1978 Canal Treaty with Jimmy Carter.

Bill Eberhard, extreme right, front row, was our biologist, and a fire balling right-hander. While Bill did not make the Hall of Fame for his baseball feats, he did for working out the seductive strategy of the famous "bolas" spider that beaned love-crazed male moths reeling them in for her repasts. Bill and I still communicate on things biological, which I do as well with his accomplished wife, Dr. Mary Jane West-Eberhard—a member of the National Academy of Science of the USA.

Chapter Eighteen

. . .

LIFE CAN BE LIKE AN UMPIRE'S CALL— YAH NEVAH KNOW

(Cali, Colombia, 1973)

The umpire cannot play our game
Too old, too infirm and slow
But the rules he doth well know
Yielding not to ardent counterclaim

'Tis our fate to play hard each game
Agile, alert, to return each blow
Yet, the ball game just might bestow
A bad bounce—never the ump to blame

Why would Mary and I take our new PhDs and move our young and growing family to a university in the so-called third world instead of advancing our careers in some exalted first world research mecca? Yes, we were young—and maybe a little reckless. But there was more to our decision than taking a thrilling dive

159

off a career high board. The upheavals of Vietnam, the civil rights movement, the assassinations (JFK/1963, MLK/1968, RFK/1968), and more, turned both of us away from conventional postdoctorals, and certainly from corporate careers. In my own case, I knew there was need in Latin America, and great potential.

Yes, I could address that need, but I realized, once in Cali, I could also scratch my baseball itch. Being a freshman scrub, a batting practice backstop on Cornell's baseball team still gnawed at me. In Cali, it seemed only natural to go out for the baseball squad of the Universidad del Valle. And, importantly, I was still determined not to perpetuate TS Eliot's dirge for April, the saddest cruellest (*sic*) month, which was really a lament for lost youth.

A beauty of baseball in the tropics is that there is no "hot stove league," no winter of dreams *under a blanket of snow* for spring's opening day. Play can start any time of year when the league is organized. Our stadium was first class, the baseball site of the 1971 Pan-Am Games. Our league operated more smoothly than the university in general: the games started on time, the field was well-maintained, the uniformed umpires always showed up, and the announcers were at the ready on a functional PA system.

We represented the "State" University of Valle (Univalle). Valle was a *departamento* in the Colombian political system. Though we played in first-class surroundings, our team was a ragtag bunch—Colombians with a smattering of Panamanians and one other gringo, a fireballing but erratic pitcher—Bill Eberhard, professor of biology. On this auspicious day, we Univalle warriors played against our archrivals from the neighboring departamento, the guys from the University of Cauca. They had not a gringo among them. We did not use the word "diversity" back then, but our "international" bunch was seriously defending the honor of Univalle borne proudly on our uniforms.

Tight game, and the fans in the stands were vivacious, vocal, and at times, vituperative. I sent them almost to the violent: I came to bat and the announcer said, *"Ahora bateando* (now batting) *José Polacco Grandí."* Weeks before, when I first heard Mamma's maiden name being broadcast, I took the first pitch with the bat on my shoulder. But this time I was focused: Came a pitch to my liking. I hit a sharp ground ball to the left side. The infielder bobbled the ball a little and rushed his throw up the first-base line. I had every right to "cream" the first baseman clearly in my path. But I didn't, stepping around him to place my toe daintily on the bag.

"Out!" yelled the umpire. I had come to know the ump because he often called balls and strikes behind me—the catcher for Univalle. So, we had developed a "relationship."

But, this time, as a base runner, I appealed.

"You gotta call interference! He was in the baseline—and I still beat the throw." To no avail.

"You're out!" His thumb went up again as he turned his back to me and walked away.

None of this was lost on the Cauca fans occupying the visitors' stands on the first-base side. "Gringo! You're out!" "Gringo, go home!" "Gringo *feo* (ugly)" And like that. They gave me no respite. There was no way I could walk or jog meekly back to our dugout on the third-base side, head bowed, under this hail of insults. Did I say I was a little reckless and adventurous? (Had I lost a lot of the insecurity of my "boy" days? Or, had I still not yet grown up?)

In the moment, I was inspired by the scene at the diamond. On our Univalle campus, our politicized student body had been providing us a very audible daily report, with commentary, of the gringo goings-on back home (and in Vietnam). The news was

161

broadcast via a sound system they set up in a central university plaza.

So, in the stadium, I put on my best Nixon facial hang-dog pout and turned to the stands to give the Cauca fans the famous double "V" sign, my jowls dancing a little. Today's commentators say the "V" is for victory, but at that time Nixon appropriated the sign from antiwar protesters, and it meant "peace."

I was not trying to pacify the crowd, of course. They dutifully went bonkers.

Only then did I return to my dugout. My teammates were laughing, calling me loco, offering me protection after the game. I accepted a victory beer on the way home, and I felt like Kid Bensonhurst.

Yes, *life is like an umpire's call.* It doesn't always go your way, but you work with what you got. Bensonhurst and the Brooklyn Dodgers taught me that.

Years later, in the beautifully fertile Missouri-Mississippi Crescent, where baseball and folklore flow into each other, Cardinals pitcher, Joaquin Andujar (*One Mean Dominican*), was being interviewed about an upcoming game. One of his answers became a baseball holy passage:

"There is one word in America that says it all, and that word is 'you never know.' "

The umpire sometimes makes the call at the most inopportune moments. November 1973, Mary and I were visiting her student's family in Cartagena, on Colombia's Atlantic coast. The occasion was the Feria de Cartagena, honoring the resistance of the "heroic city" to English privateers' attempts at a takeover and confiscation of gold leaving the Spanish Main.

(Privateers were pirates hired by the English crown, yes, to steal the Spaniards' stolen gold. What bloody nerve!)

The scene was chaotically *costeño* (the Atlantic coast): beauty pageants, parades with both classical and more "popular" floats, fireworks, cross-dressing, dangerous street firecrackers that detonated at our feet, and charcoal-darkened afro-colombianos in loin cloths making pointed appeals for "contributions" with their homemade spears. It was all creative mayhem to a tropical beat.

Of course, there was also dancing, and Mary and I loved to dance. Mary has Teutonic features, but she danced like a Latina. Even at the worst, the catcalls were "*cachaco/a*," or dancing like an uptight resident of Bogotá (or the highlands, in cold contrast to the humid, pulsating Atlantic coast.) For Americans, being called a *cachaco* was a compliment: we did not dance like gringos.

We were at a *caseta*—a fancy tent: Think of a spirited revival tent in the deep, American South, but what moved our souls here was live music (cumbia, bolero, vallenato, paso doble, etc.), and it never stopped. A band would play its whole repertoire until the next band on the program seamlessly took over, no such thing as a break. We were at a table with some friends of Mary's student, when our favorite cumbia came on.

"Let's dance. They're playing our song." Yes, I was full of original lines.

"No."

"No?" I retorted in disbelief. It was only two a.m. or so.

"No, I don't want to," she replied, with resolve.

"Did I get you mad at me?"

"I'm pregnant."

Well, that put the kibosh on the evening. We were taken back to the house of Mary's student's brother-in-law, a successful banker who was hosting us.

So, we learned of Benjamin John, our third, who we would smuggle back to the US in late December, a Christmas present for Mamma Vina. (The package content was revealed July 1, 1974.)

Do the crazy stuff when you're young. Somehow, boring life gets more precious when you're old.

SEXY MISS BOLAS SPIDER
A tribute to Bill Eberhard's field work.

From: *A Life's Rambles/Ramblas de una vida* (Joe Polacco, 2021)

She pitches at night, hanging from a thread
and playing out a sticky hanging ball
at a love-crazed moth, seeking a newlywed
Yay, her faux perfume has him in thrall

She's a spider "lady of the night," y'all
You can just call her Señorita Bolas
She puts a *lil' extry* on the ball
and emits a scent—*tropical Gladiolus*

Inflamed macho mothro flies upstream
beckoned by the infuriating bouquet
He notes not the swinging ball-peen
until it beans him on his love-lorn way

Males oft bring gifts to their beloveds
but Moth you'll have no babies with Miss Bolas
Tis your calories for her spiderlings she covets
Tough nature has taught you what your role is

Chapter Nineteen

• • •

A BROOKLYN WASTELAND
(ca. 1976)

> Humankind delivers daily detritus
> And brethren, our business is booming
> We have the touch of a negative Midas:
> Turning solids to waste and liquids a-fuming
>
> Our filth is a byproduct of ambition
> Hell-bent to fulfil our lot to advance
> In our waste lots reeking of perdition
> Satan calls his angels' *contredanse*

After Cali, I spent about nine months at Brookhaven National Laboratories as a postdoctoral associate. Then, in late August 1974, I began my first permanent American job as a staff scientist at the Connecticut Agricultural Experiment Station (CAES) in New Haven. Mary was awarded a very competitive NIH postdoctoral research fellowship at Yale. We first-time homeowners became a young family of five about two months before our arrival in New Haven: Benjamin, b. July 1, 1974 (Patchogue, Long Island, NY); Joseph, b. July 25, 1972 (Cali, Colombia); Laura, b. January 17, 1970 (Durham, NC). Mary and I were able to do what we loved—experimental science. And we were able to make our mortgage payments (on top of Stepdad's largesse with the down payment).

After two years in distant Cali, we took advantage of our new proximity to Brooklyn and Long Island to visit our children's grandparents on many weekends. Stepdad Lou was proud to say, "Every time you come in you will see improvements." Yes, things were looking up, literally. Mamma and Lou bought the two-story building that housed the linoleum store and were aiming to move to the upstairs apartment—still on 86th Street, and closer to the noisy, elevated, West End, but a definite improvement in privacy and living quarters.

The move, however, required heavy renovation. Stepdad and his son Louis ("Sonny"—every Italian family has one) were well versed in building trades—plumbing, electrical wiring, carpentry, masonry, flooring—and I am leaving out auto mechanics and TV repair. The Italian genome seems to have many DIY *loci* if I may be technical. Our building was old, and the renovation generated much scrap: plaster, moulding, flooring, plumbing fixtures, electrical wiring, and outlets, etc. The junk seemed to be self-propagating and had to be jettisoned. It called for a trip to the dump.

At the time, New York City had a world-famous dump in Staten Island—Fresh Kills, a lovely name for a ghastly massive assault on Mother Nature. It occupied an area equivalent to two and a half Central Parks and became a rookery for those flying, feathered cockroaches—sea gulls—plus hordes of other terrestrial garbage feeders and scavengers. It seeped a distillate of brown-black vile-smelling fluid. Staten Islanders proudly claimed that the dump could be seen from outer space. Mercifully, it was closed in 2001, covered with plastic tarp, incinerator ash and then many tons of soil from the Jersey Pine Barrens. After two decades it is almost beautiful, with new "hills" and a variety of plant and animal life. It generates methane that is captured to warm home and hearth in the neighborhood.

But we did not participate in this urban recycling experiment. Our debris went to a place in Brooklyn. I am almost sure of this because Stepdad could not travel to Staten Island. He was psychologically restrained from traveling out of Brooklyn, and I know we didn't cross the Verrazzano Bridge. Not to worry, Sonny knew of a place in Brooklyn. To me it was extensive, dotted with low wattage "street" lamps, evoking a hybrid moonscape and an HP Lovecraft type of wasteland, devoid of human life. (Though the spirits of some of Sal La Puma's fedora victims may have frequented it to stay close to Bensonhurst.)

While unloading our cargo, a thin, nervous guy in civvies and a tie showed up, asking for our dumping permit. We came up empty-handed, and lame excuses did not work. He identified himself as an officer of the City of New York Department of Sanitation and proceeded to write us a summons. He was crouched, concentrating on his pad of summons forms on his knee, when Sonny suggested something that included the word "palm." This was New York-ese for a bribe, making a payoff to avoid a much larger and more damaging fine. The official looked up and said something like: "Don't ask me. I didn't hear it, and now everybody's clean." This was during a periodic cleansing of corruption in New York. Just our rotten luck.

Then things got weird. Sonny was a firefighter, a fellow municipal employee, and tried to use his FDNY connection to get off. No dice. The sanitation guy went back to writing on his form pad, and Sonny was fuming. He told his dad that he could just clobber the guy over the head with an old pipe or two-by-four and bury him under the trash. No one would be the wiser. I believed he was serious, and I could not believe that the crouched official did not hear him. Stepdad gave his son a look—he could be very calming and reasonable at times of impending insanity or horrible judgment. He nodded a "no" and signaled Sonny to stay cool, his palm patting an imaginary child on the head. We got our ticket and left, and I do not recall if we finished unloading our cargo—after all, we had "paid" for the privilege. All the way back to 86th Street, Sonny was still *kvetching.* Yes, Italians could do that, this is Bensonhurst, after all.

Soon after, Mary and I drove our family back to New Haven. On our next visit to Bensonhurst, I asked Stepdad about the aborted dumping operation. With a smirk rising from each side of his mouth he smugly intimated that he just did the natural thing. He had gone to a meeting of a local Democratic Club and asked a judge for a favor; no specifics were raised. I wasn't there, of course, but I could see the judge giving him an almost imperceptible nod. Stepdad told me he inserted the summons in the judge's pocket (which one? overcoat? pants?), and the problem just went away. Oh yes, Sonny and Stepdad said that the sanitation official in the wasteland was notorious for "being on the take," but we picked the wrong time to dump illegally. Just our rotten luck in the dump.

Twelve years of public education, four of college, five-plus of grad school, two years as a university prof, almost a year's postdoctoral, and about two years as a research scientist did not teach lessons that covered what I learned that night in the Brooklyn wasteland.

La Puma's Boys could have told me that.

Chapter Twenty

• • •

I ALMOST TOOK THE CAKE
(Columbia, MO, 1980)

The cerebral steed grows ever stronger
But must self-rein its stupid impulses
The horse sees the finish line no longer
If blinded by rage and perceived injustice

Do we reach maturity brick by quid
As if building a personal pyramid?
Or is manhood reached via perilous trek
Along the way avoiding the big wreck?

Alternative chapter title, "How did I grow up?" This little bit of biography could have been the intro to my obituary.

Five years had passed in Connecticut; that phase of our professional lives was over. I looked forward to combining teaching and research at the University of Missouri (MU), and to have more independence in both. MU (Mizzou) showed encouraging interest in Mary. I got the job, and she got separate lab space and independence in research.

We arrived in Columbia, Missouri, late August 1979. I was a thirty-five-year-old new professor with a strong competitive spirit, dedicated to the long struggle . . . so different from others' opinion of me, and my own self-perception, in the Bensonhurst of my boyhood. However, though I thought long-term, my temper was still decidedly short.

I had indeed arrived at this new persona. In my previous job, I was an outspoken critic of the administration of my research institute, New Haven's CAES, oldest Experiment Station in the US and second oldest in the world. Over my five years there, I accomplished enough, and impressed (if not charmed) enough folks, to land a faculty position at MU (good ole Mizzou).

At the CAES, I dealt with frustrating limitations in funding and research freedom, and at Mizzou, I dealt with new frustrations. Before I arrived, Schweitzer Hall, the building that was to house my lab, was shut down because of radioactive contamination (going back to the days when Mizzou provided Marie and Pierre Curie with the radioactive isotopes found in Missouri pitchblende). Decontamination of Schweitzer was slow, and renovation was just a pipe dream. My chairman, an ally of mine, quit in protest.

"Next year in Jerusalem."

As my frustrations mounted, I came off as an "in-your-face" guy; one driven to make a career mark. My East Coast chutzpah and lack of diplomacy clashed with Midwest sensibilities/sensitivities. We arrived in Columbia well before 9/11/2001—that is, well before the nation realized that New Yorkers really were Americans.

July 25, 1980: I'd been in Missouri about eleven months. I know the date because it was number one son Joseph's eighth birthday. I ordered an ice-cream cake at a Baskin-Robbins branch at a major intersection (Providence Ave. and Broadway Blvd. for locals who care to know). I had paid for the cake when making the order. When I came back to pick it up, the staff was new (to me). I dealt with a young lady who refused to hand over the cake because there was no record of my having paid. I nearly blew a gasket, remonstrating (putting it politely), and putting the young lady in a difficult spot. She held fast. I left in a rage, got into my van, and took off.

Waiting for a light to change at that same intersection, I saw police flashers in my rearview mirror. Grumbling audible obscenities, I impulsively jumped out of my beat-up red van (with a junkyard replacement white rear door). My anger was obvious as I slammed the driver-side door. My anger was still obvious as I approached the police officer who was already out of his patrol car. I could see the surprise on his face. I am thankful now he did not escalate the situation.

Calmly, he informed me that I was in line for a bunch of fines: Driving with EXPIRED Connecticut license plates, and without a Missouri driver's license as he soon learned. He also claimed that I did not have a Missouri state automobile inspection. Aha! That I did, and the decal on my windshield proved it.

So, still calmly, he said that I was looking at costly fines and a hassle. I paraphrase his response: "Tell you what. You get those Missouri plates and license, call me at this number (on his card), and we are good."

Mollified, I thanked him and was on my way. I changed the plates, updated to a Missouri driver's license, and left a message with the officer. Earlier, I had profusely apologized to Madam

Manager at the Baskin-Robbins. She let me down easy. I told her she had a very competent and loyal employee, and that Joseph had a wonderful birthday celebration with his new friends and a special ice cream cake. (And, Joe, *stunad*, hold on to the receipt!)

Considering many current incidents, I count at least three major circumstances that were blessings in disguise. I came out on the positive side of "what ifs?"

What if I were brown or Black, jumping out of my beat up van approaching a police car, and with obvious anger and consternation on my face?

What if it were nighttime darkness, especially a night of unrest in Columbia? We have had many since then.

What if the officer were not so restrained and disciplined?

I was taller then, and more buff, with a summer tan, and could have been perceived as more threatening or dangerous. I had just turned thirty-six and was in much better shape than this doddering late seventy-year-old example of human senescence.

I acted like one of La Puma's Bensonhurst Boys might have, and I know I retained the neighborhood accent. However, it was a hot midsummer day, and my T-shirt and shorts lessened the possibility of my carrying a concealed weapon. And guns were not as common in downtown Columbia as they are now.

All of the above is small retrospective comfort. Not everyone can count on those circumstantial advantages. This incident was important in the "Midwestification" of an East Coaster, one who did not become another statistic.

I was growing from "boy" to "man-child." Indeed, reprints of the many scientific papers I pushed and proudly published over my professional years are now in a large looseleaf binder, gathering dust in a corner of my home office. In overall scientific progress, the advances they made are increasingly smaller steps, soon to be ground into the mortar of the science edifice. I comfort myself in the assurance that even if Galileo, Darwin, Einstein, and other giants never lived, science would stand pretty much where it does today.

I'm dangerously close to sermonizing by asserting that it is science we should extol and not individuals in the trade. From "my works," I mostly value the wonderful collaborations with colleagues and students. Tributes to some are in my poetic collection: *A Life's Rambles/Ramblas de una vida*. This is not a shameless plug; scientists always cite themselves.

Though at first a driven scientist at Mizzou, I mellowed over time: Fun interactions in the classroom and lab did not hinder "productivity," indeed they even facilitated it.

I had been at Mizzou almost 20 years, and I learned to make learning fun, such as lip-syncing Tony Bennet ("The Best is Yet to Come") as the class performed a dance routine for bacterial transformation: (Fall, 1997 *Mizzou Magazine*. Article by Jane Latus Musick, Photo by Nancy O'Connor).

I realized that soirees at the Oriental Manor and Cotillion Terrace were an important part of my professional training.

Sal La Puma inspired this story.

Two "Evil" (or at least absorbed) scientists mugging it up, Polacco on left cutting DNA, and Dale Blevins of Agronomy Dept. with captive roots.

Chapter Twenty-One

• • •

BENSONHURST MAN-CHILD IN BOSTON
(or BAHston, yer cherce/your choice, 1989–1990)

No Sabbath Rest on Sabbatical. A radical change in the environment is like stepping almost back to boyhood and then stepping forward and growing up all over again. I recommend the humility that comes with placing yourself in a situation where you are not the boss, if only temporarily. I eventually chose Boston as the site of my first sabbatical. "Beantowners" are part of the US (they would say the origin), but they have unique outlooks that they readily express and in different dialect.

I was at the University of Missouri nine years before venturing out on my first sabbatical. Don't cry for me. It wasn't as if I were chained to my post. There was the question of gaining tenure ('79 to '85), coordinating with Mary about the institutions of the sabbatical, and then applying for the leave. Settling on a location for the sabbatical was a great illustration of the differences of our planning approaches—I plan, Mary dives headfirst.

I was methodically dividing the country into regions, with their cultural outlets, and desirable labs. By these metrics, Boston was in the top echelon. Early in the process, I had an invitation from Gerry Fink to join his lab at the Massachusetts Institute of Technology (MIT). I zipped across the hall to give Mary the news of the possibility, and within an hour she returned to my office telling me she had set up a sabbatical in Ann Simon's lab at the University of Massachusetts in Amherst, 90 miles from Cambridge.

The wheels of academia can grind slowly, but by spring semester 1988, I was approved for a salaried year, and Mary was set up in Amherst. We had Mass covered east to west. In the east, Cambridge's extramural features included great seafood, the Italian North End, Boston Garden (a site for Cornell hockey), the Sox at Fenway, and the Jazz Boat and Aquarium in the Boston Harbor. The list is not exhaustive. Western Mass was lovely and exciting in its own right, and it offered our youngest, Ben, an invigorating and "coming out" year at Amherst HS where our baby became de MAN. (Certainly more the man than I was at the same age.) He was a soccer and wrestling standout, and popular with several young ladies.

But Ben was also *our* baby again, the only child living with us. Leaving his older brother, Joseph, in Columbia for his high school senior year was tough on all, but it worked out. Joseph grew up as well. He lived with our good buddy, Jerry Lucchesi, and Jerry's son Allan, Joseph's soccer teammate. Laura, our oldest, was a sophomore at Cal-Berkeley. Our reunions over holiday and semester breaks were sweet.

Of course, we embarked on the sabbatical for the science, which was fantastic, much more than we had hoped for. I was at MIT's Whitehead Institute, the 1982 product of a well-strategized

$130 million gift from industrialist Edwin C. "Jack" Whitehead. "Strategized?" By the end of my stay in 1990, Philadelphia's Institute for Scientific Information named the Whitehead "the top research institution in the world in molecular biology and genetics" (https://wi.mit.edu/history). My presence had nothing to do with that rating, though I am happy to entertain contrary arguments.

I joined the lab of Gerry Fink, Brooklyn-born and proud basketball alum of Amherst College. Gerry left Cornell after fifteen productive years to join MIT/Whitehead at its founding. He was prescient. I entered a laboratory of wonderful colleagues who were *all-around* stars: well-read and interesting intellectuals, athletes, dancers, martial artists, et al.—just good and fun people. I shared a bench with a young Cornell alum who at times clogged around the lab in wooden shoes. His dad was a Swedish scientist who co-discovered the Wood-Ljungdahl pathway, which naturally generates much of the acetate in the biosphere. (Please don't scoff. Nitrogen and carbon cycles are essential for life on earth.) That I was the son of a sweatshop seamstress and a Bensonhurst linoleum salesman did not matter. Others in the lab came from blue-collar backgrounds. They did not look down on Bensonhurst. Boston had its own versions, and some of their émigrés populated the hallowed faculty halls of MIT and Harvard.

My academic year at MIT was far from unremitting academic drudgery. There was the MIT softball league, weekly noontime pickup basketball, or lunchtime jogging/running through Cambridge or across the Charles River, nature outings, a fortnightly lab meeting that went on all morning amid scientific fireworks (and *great* food), and more. The institute-wide Friday happy hour featured Boston's finest brews, some of which came from the Fink lab's brewmeisters.

I know I'm making the Whitehead sound like a year-round recreational camp for young scientists. But, the Fink lab *produced*, driven by efficiency, two superb lab managers, and the wonderful congeniality of its twenty-five to thirty hardworking and gifted members, who also worked nights and weekends.

I could have been intimidated by the consistently high intellectual level of my colleagues. There is still a tinnitus of doubt ringing in my *capo dosto*, for example, that my passing grade on the Stuyvesant HS entrance exam was due to a clerical error. My insecurity could have kicked in at the Whitehead, but it did not. The exchange of ideas was stimulating, challenging, but nonthreatening. Incredibly, I had something to offer, and not just a cerebral hard drive of baseball stats and stars. Some lab mates worked on the model plant *Arabidopsis*—the rest on yeast genetics, with much interaction between the two groups. Since I was a plant scientist with a PhD in fungal genetics, I had a foot in both areas, and that synergy very much helped my own research program back in Missouri.

To most lab mates, I compared favorably with a professor of renown who had earlier taken full advantage of his MIT-Whitehead sabbatical to attend every cultural event in the Boston area. To me, the sabbatical was not a cultural Valhalla as much as an opportunity to become a more productive scientist.

Boston was "something else." Just as North Carolinians thought much more about those Yankee Northerners than we Northerners did of them, Bostonians seemed fixated on comparing themselves—favorably, of course—to smug New Yorkers. (Recall that in 1990 the Curse of the Bambino was still casting its spell: My *New York* Mets won the 1986 World Series over the Sox in miraculous fashion.) Despite my New York heritage, accent, and leanings, and my science creds, I got along well with the maintenance staff of the institute (as I did at the CAES). I wish I could have put that on my résumé. I just put it in this book hoping that it gets read by a few.

Boston was gastronomically enriching for this Italian kid from Bensonhurst. A tidbit: Mangia Calamari/The Daily Catch of the North End served stuffed calamari appetizer, linguine with clams in white sauce, black (squid ink) linguine with minced calamari *aglio olio* sauce, and more (save room for cannoli and *sfogliatelle* dessert). Seating was limited, so our family was obliged to sit almost in the kitchen and to share our table with strangers, who became our friends. More than once, our waitress/cook ran out to the street to play a number. Except for the accents this could have been my Bensonhurst.

My ninety-plus mile Amherst to Boston commute was ameliorated by wonderful scenery changing with the season, and by overnighting twice a week with brother-in-law George and family in Worcester, Massachusetts (WOO-stermass). On Fridays, I'd take a round trip on the Amherst-Boston "party bus" full of eager partygoers, mostly females. So, Mary had the family van over three-day weekends.

Stressors we did endure, "No Sabbath Rest." I list them not for pity but to look back and recall how they pulled us together as a family:

Hostile tenants (a law student and his wife), back in Columbia. They were renting our house while we were on the East Coast. They sued us for a house that wasn't "rental ready." Hey, we were a family of five: two professionals, a kid in college and two in high school. They moved in with appliances and a lot of furniture—no need. As a result of the flap, we drove 1,250-miles back to Columbia for a deposition and some serious home cleanup and yardwork. Other collateral damage was legal costs and much *agita*, like hosting in Amherst two cats that were supposed to have remained in our Columbia home. Then the whole affair was dropped, by the plaintiffs I presume.

Paco, the blue and gold macaw unknown to the rental agent. We secreted Paco from Missouri to Massachusetts. He did become popular, however, with local schoolkids whom he serenaded as they passed under his second-floor aerie. One late fall afternoon Paco flew off our deck, and our secret was out, all over town, including local Amherst radio. Paco came back, eventually. I even missed a lab Monday because of this family crisis.

The Bay Area 1989 World Series earthquake while Laura was attending Cal. I was trying to catch the third game of the World Series while driving back from Cambridge and heard the stress in the voices of the sportscasters. This could not be good. Mary was at a meeting out of state; hence my anxiety was unbridled.

I was scared for Laura at Berkeley, and unnerved by lack of information. A newscaster advised folks not to call the Bay Area so as not to tie up the lines, but sonuvagun, he was chatting with his brother in San Francisco, *on the air*. When I tried to call, Ben was on our phone with his girlfriend, until I kicked him off. Laura answered right away: She was at marching band practice and giggled how the ground moved to accommodate one of her marching steps. She inherited her father's sense of humor.

We lived in a swampy area, not far from Emily Dickinson's grave. The grave was not a problem, but we advised Ben not to step on it on his way to skate on an iced-over pond. One spring weekend, the electricity went out and without our sump pump our basement became a swamp extension. We had a "sub-tenant," a mellow ex-footballer from Mizzou, who was in a graduate program at UMass. I still picture him walking in ankle-deep water in the basement. I don't think he was in electrical engineering. (He arranged his rental with the same agency that handled ours, his Missouri origin a pure coincidence I believe.)

Through all this we came together. Stressors can cause family fissures, but we came through, stronger for confronting adversity. I was always happy to get back from Cambridge to our Amherst home on Friday evenings—usually going eye-to-eye with an airborne Paco as I opened the front door—when Mary had a wonderful fish/seafood dinner ready. Mary was much more than a housewife and mom—her research project at UMass–Amherst went well enough to earn her an invitation to present a seminar at the Whitehead.

Oh yes, there are regrets, one of the biggest was not taking my ailing car to Tom and Ray Magliozzi's *Car Talk* garage. What was I thinking? (Dope slap.) That would have been a little like Bensonhurst in Cambridge, their fair city.

> A lot of New England did we roam
> Our list so inspired, became a poem
> Ahhh, there was Berkshire Skiing
> And Ella Fitzgerald's Tanglewood singing

Four seasons I loved, some more than others
So, I retroactively express my druthers
For woods to hike, mountains to bike
With so much to love, what's to dislike?

And young Ben off the rasslers' scale
I'd greet with cannoli, his will to impale
But his making weight I did not usurp:
We hit on high-protein clams to schlurp

We grew up together, family and I
From cool episodes to things gone awry
For we carried back to the Show-Me State
Myriad spores of change to germinate

Why "man-child" instead of "man" in this chapter's title? I grew up some more in New England. One needs to relocate to note where the fabric of manhood needs darning and alterations—the alterations were in my improved understanding of the difficulty of research, especially under a demanding advisor.

I also better understood Mary's difficult situation, and the darning was in the mesh of my responsibility to her. Mary learned late in our Amherst stay of an adverse employment situation in Missouri. She initiated a labor grievance that eventually became a lawsuit against the university and its Department of Biochemistry (hence, against my chairman). I tried to navigate the narrow lane between being Mary's loyal husband and a good departmental citizen. Back in Missouri, I was deposed by university lawyers, and was a witness at Mary's federal trial in spring 1993, examined by lawyers representing either Mary or the university.

While we had high points, it was clear we were taking divergent paths, at home and professionally. Mary's professional life in Missouri became a deep national/international involvement in maize (corn) genetics and genomics, and home life centered around our new place outside Columbia, with its greenhouse, and its vineyard overlooking the Missouri River. Fishing became big for Mary, and she went off with Columbia friends on regular "fish camps" near Branson in Southern Missouri. I attended at least one, which was indeed fun.

Yet, not long after my Spanish sabbatical, we separated and eventually divorced in 2005. This was the major "spore of change" that we carried back to Columbia, Missouri from Boston.

66 *In Brooklyn, it was as*
though you were in your
own little bubble. You
were all part of one big,
but very close family, and
the Dodgers were the
main topic of everybody's
conversations and you
could sense the affection
people had for you. 99

—Don Drysdale

PART III

Bensonhurst Man

(2000 to the Present)

While my travels took me well beyond boyhood and Bensonhurst, the bonds to the old neighborhood in fact are not broken, but now moor my manhood.

66 *I once started out
to walk around the
world but ended up in
Brooklyn, that Bridge
was too much
for me.* 99

—Lawrence Ferlinghetti

Chapter Twenty-Two

• • •

BENSONHURST MAN IN SPAIN
(2000–2001)

What does Spain have to do with Bensonhurst, already?

Everything, when it comes to Bensonhurst's Latino, Jewish and Italian populations. The interwoven strands are complex and I do not claim mastery of history.

Let's start with Italian and Iberian culture, history, and language. The cultures are inextricably intertwined and bundled, and they extend to the old 'hood. Who's the better tenor, Plácido Domingo or Luciano Pavarotti? Cured ham? Yer cherce: *jamón serrano* vs prosciutto. What of chorizo vs salsiccia, *gambas al ajillo* vs shrimp scampi, manchego vs pecorino romano, paella vs risotto, Spanish omelet vs *frittata*? Well, what of it/them? They are conjugate stars in parallel universes, Spain vs Italy.

We love to mistrust and complain about the other, from olive oil to soccer to history: After centuries of battles against the Carthaginians and native peoples, Rome conquered the Iberian Peninsula in 197 BC. Rome left a language, temples, aqueducts, etc., but almost seventeen centuries later, Spain (Aragon) turned the tables in Naples and Sicily (1443), and ruled for a couple of centuries. (My very loose time line is just to show that Spaniards and Italians have a "history.")

And, some Jewish history, of course, is embedded in Spanish history. The Catholic kings, Ferdinand and Isabel, expelled the remaining Moorish rulers from Granada, Spain in 1492, the same year they financed Columbus' voyages that wound up "discovering" the New World.

For our discussion, Sephardic Jews were expelled from Spain that same year of 1492. After some higher-order diasporas, many Jews (mostly Ashkenazi) settled in Bensonhurst, living cheek to jowl with Italian victims of the Austrians and later the independent Italian north. Brooklyn also had a population of "Syrian Jews," the local term for the Sephardim. So, by different routes and circumstances, Jews and Italians cohabited Bensonhurst.

I hasten to add that Italians never suffered an unspeakable holocaust, such as unleashed by Nazism on Jews, nor even the "minor" pogroms perpetrated on Jews over much of European history, going back to the Crusades and earlier.

For me, however, Spain was an ineluctable draw. So, I did it again—I moved to Spain of 2000, my new country, sight unseen. It's not that modern Spain was an unknown quantity; my good MU buddies, Professors Dave Emerich, Dale Blevins, and Judy Wall, had lovely collaborations there. The link between Dave and Spanish Prof Tomás Ruiz-Argüeso was especially strong, at professional and family levels. I had read Washington Irving's *Tales of the Alhambra* and Cervantes's *Don Quijote de La Mancha*. Culturally, I was prepared to know Spain close-up, but I got too close, falling in love with it—like finding love in an *arranged marriage*, despite your new mate's idiosyncrasies.

My arranged marriage with Spain was in the context of science and culture. I was still married to Mary, who stayed in Columbia. She had won parts of a gender discrimination suit against MU and the Biochemistry Department. Though she could have remained in biochemistry, she took on a new job as curator of the national maize genome database centered in the USDA unit on campus. She showed amazing fortitude at taking on this new position in a different department and in a field for which she was not trained. And, she branched out to enology, establishing and managing her vineyard at our new home. She visited me in Spain, October 2000. We barnstormed south to north: Granada (El Alhambra), Madrid, Rio del Duero wine country, and beautiful Hondarribia in Basque country on the Biscay coast. We truly had a wonderful time.

I was in Madrid for a Fulbright-sponsored research fellowship in the lab of Tomás Ruiz-Argüeso. Just as Bensonhurst and Boston have their own English, Madrid has its own even more extreme Spanish, and theirs is codified in tremendous tomes from *La Real Academia Española*, dating back to 1780—164 years after Cervantes's death. *Extreme* Spanish? They did "invent" the language, so don't laugh when they lisp.

On Madrid's streets, I learned to ask directions clearly and slowly, or the immediate response was a scornful "eeehhhhh?" (Translation*: He walks and talks like a tourist.*) I knew I was adapting when metro "bird chirping" became snippets of intelligible conversation.

There were aspects of life in Madrid that required adaptation. I list three here. One was accepting that pedestrians in Madrid did not confine themselves to the right lane. They slid past each other. In Bensonhurst, we young studs sporting our high school football jackets of honor did not yield to oncoming rivals. Shoulder clashes were common. We didn't walk the sidewalks, we patrolled our lanes, like individual Pumas. Madrileños avoided contact with a beautiful sidewalk fandango.

Cigarette smoke was pervasive in Madrid, even on underground metro platforms that sported "No Smoking" signs, on ashtrays of all places. [A doctor friend gave a tri-partite defense of subway smoking: *(i)* It's "cute" *(mono)*, reflecting the rebellious Spanish nature. *(ii)* And what about car exhaust? *(iii)* And there are bigger fish to fry, e.g., Basque terrorism.] Say what you will about New York subways, and a lot could be said, but smoking prohibitions are generally followed.

Madrid sidewalks were peppered with dog poop. (Supposedly, Paris was even worse in this regard.) I never thought that Bensonhursters would pick up after their dogs, even "curbing" was too much to ask, but they do it now. I believe that Madrid also eventually came around.

Overall, though, the positives of Madrid and Spain well outweighed the drawbacks during my stay.

My first academic activity was the Fourth European (Biological) Nitrogen Fixation Conference in Sevilla (September 16–20, 2000), where I presented a poster and met future colleagues. The Ruiz-Argüeso lab covered my meeting registration fee and hotel room. I had a single room, while new lab mates/ colleagues Drs. Juan Imperial and Pepe Palacios doubled up in another. (No, their last names did not make it a royal suite.)

A word from scientist Joe: Biological Nitrogen Fixation, the conference theme, may not seem of paramount importance, but there is no way our world could feed eight billion folks if not for half of our fertilizer nitrogen coming from energy-intensive industrial conversion of nitrogen gas to ammonium. For reasons of renewable energy use and security, we need to improve solar-driven fixation of N_2—biological or industrial. Security? The downstream industrial fertilizer product, ammonium nitrate, is also a powerful explosive. Recall the devastating accidental 2020 Beirut port explosion, and the intentional 1995 bombing of the Alfred P. Murrah Federal Building in Oklahoma City.

The conference "local culture" night started with a one-hour bus ride south to Jerez de la Frontera and the Tío Pepe distillery, producers of fine Jerez. Well, the English call it sherry, but they get it from Spain. The Brits are lovingly jingoistic; Giovanni Caboto is "John Cabot," and Nicaragua is "Nicka ROG-oo-ah," and so on. But ya gotta love 'em, and I digress. (I think the Spanish never got over the defeat of the Invincible Armada, and some of that resentment may have rubbed off on me.)

I mention this evening outing to make a point—yes, it is coming. The evening included a royal horse show and a sumptuous meal in a large, ornate banquet hall. The sherry and cider were fantastic and flowing, and the flamenco demo out of this world. When volunteers were called up, some intrepid Germans jumped on the stage, but soon the floor in front was inundated with dancing conferees.

What a night! We danced almost till dawn, but the sun did indeed rise over our bus returning to Sevilla. No one slept. There was a mixed chorus of different languages discussing science and whatever. As we pulled up to our hotel, some folks offered to buy a nightcap.

I can really work here, I thought: *This is a spirited crowd, passionate about the science of life and about life in general.*

And that is my point: I concluded I was in the right place and in the right discipline.

Yes, Spanish science, history, culture, and cuisine that I experienced were awesome. But, "my Spanish Family" made Spain my new neighborhood, my Bensonhurst. Pondering how to capsulize it all, I see tales of at least four branches of "my Spanish family." I am only skimming the surfaces of my relationships with them and with others, who could fill a list of blockbuster movie credits:

i. Alicia's parents. Alicia Rodriguez was my competent, conscientious, and charming lab technician at MU. Before, during, and after my sabbatical, she was in Columbia, MO with husband Miguel, a doctoral student in agronomy. I connected with Alicia's parents, gracious hosts Pepe, retired detective from the Madrid police force, and Alicia, retired hairdresser. Pepe had his route of tapas bars (off the tourist beat). We usually made quick stops at each—I think to show as many buddies as possible his daughter's American boss. Just like on 86th Street, the guys all seemed to share a secret.

Pepe and Alicia's apartment for Sunday dinner was like visiting my *paesani* on Bensonhurst Sundays, and I brought pastries. And once, I could offer Pepe and Alicia my own Bensonhurst traveling delegate, my visiting Mamma Vina (December 2000). We invited Pepe and Alicia over for an Italian seafood repast in my apartment in a humble working-class neighborhood (*Mirasierra*—86th Street without the El, but with noisy streets, nearby market stalls, courtyard clotheslines and views into neighbors' kitchens). Pepe, Alicia, Mamma, and I got along famously, and famously communicated—Italian dialect, broken English, and a variety of Spanish all around—*just* like 86th.

A cultural difference: Alicia's younger sister, Andrea, was dating a boy, almost a steady, but he was not invited upstairs until he made a firmer commitment. So, he phoned ahead and met her downstairs on the street. Strict it was, but there was *no* curfew. Andrea came home whenever, often at dawn, and transportation from the *discotecas* was provided by "the Owl," a minibus that dragged a net to retrieve youngsters from night spots all over town. Her folks were sound asleep upon her arrival. (Mamma Vina would have said, "But they have *clear* heads." She could say that in Spanish.)

Cultural connections: Mamma was right at home with the open-air markets, again just like 86th. She observed a guy filleting a beautiful sole, and exclaimed, "Now there's a guy who loves his work." She was rewarded with the bones of certain fish that made the best broth.

I had a relaxed relationship with entrepreneurs at the markets. For example, in Madrid, deep sea flounder, sole, is *gallo*, which more commonly translates to "rooster." I kidded my fishmonger buddy that I wanted a flounder fresh enough to have crowed that morning. He took out a specimen he presented as Plácido Domingo. These are the kinds of interactions that occurred in Joe's Fish Market across from our linoleum store on 86th Street.

ii. Tomás Ruiz-Argüeso and his lovely, loving Carmina. Carmina and Tomás were an important part of my extended family in Madrid. The photo of them on the following page, with the sun setting in the background over a large body of water, captures the alluring fusion and contrasts of the Iberian Peninsula. The couple embodies the cranky kaleidoscopic unity that is Spain—Carmina's Arabic/Sephardic/Romani Andalucian South, and Tomás' more Gaelic North of Castilla y León—the land of Cervantes' La Mancha. Carmina and Tomás have three beautiful children and a bevy of *nietos*/grandchildren.

The photo was not taken against a backdrop of the Mediterranean or the Bay of Biscay. Rather, it was Lake Ontario (2001) where Tomás and I attended the Thirteenth International N-Fixation Conference in Hamilton, Ontario. I felt so much at home with them, be it in their Madrid apartment, their country home in the Sierra de Madrid (Cerceda), on the Missouri campus, or in Hamilton, Ontario. I treasured spending Holy Week at Tomás's ancestral home in Villamol (Province of León, Castilla y León). On Easter Sunday, we witnessed the Pasos de Cristo procession by religious "guilds" in Sahagún, and a family lunch in this Capital of Leeks.

Spain, like Bensonhurst, is many things—history, people, colleagues, but in this chapter I dwell on three friends now lost. Carmina and Tomás were two of them and part of my Spanish family. They embody some of the patchwork unity that is Spain: The arabic/sephardic/gypsy Andalucian South (Carmina), and Tomás's more Gaelic North of Castilla y León, of Cervantes' La Mancha.

I always thought Italians were "kissy-face," but I witnessed amazing buccal greetings within Tomás's family. Come on now, tell me, when a twelve-year-old boy walks ten table places to plant one on his uncle's *faccia*, now that is serious kissy-face, no? Would I see that at the Paradise Ballroom or the Cotillion Terrace? Maybe, in the very old days when we channeled Louis Prima and Frankie Lane at the mic and threw sandwiches to each other (*The Jilted Groom [1940]*).

Speaking of special family get-togethers, Tomás and Carmina would never let me spend *Noche Vieja*/New Year's Eve alone in Madrid. They had MANY (one hundred?) friends and relatives over in their apartment, and I was one—I felt so accepted, thank you. I think I even helped in the kitchen, but I don't recall what I did (peel my roasted peppers?).

No way I could swallow a grape at each of the twelve strokes of midnight, but my rookie status saved me from being penalized.

St. Valentine's Day (2001) massacre? I announced a presentation to each of the ladies of Tomás's lab, regaling them individually with chocolates and the promise of a poem. At the appointed hour, a nimbus of angels in white lab gowns rose upstairs to our library. They sat around a large table, looking dark darts at me. My heart was pounding. *Will I die up here? Am I breaking some Spanish code of propriety, respect, and chivalry?* I read one of my recycled poems, "My Argentine Fantasy." More silence, and more piercing looks. Then, a few sighs, and applause. They *loved* it.

News of the event made its way to Tomás, who proudly described it to colleagues.

A few years later, Dale Blevins, Dave Emerich and I attended yet another European N-fixation meeting, this time the Eleventh, in Tenerife, Canary Islands (2014). It was organized by Pepe Palacios, setting the stage for a surprise farewell to Tomás on his pending retirement. Dave gave a wonderful description of his first farewell to lab mate Tomás at the University of Oregon, many years before. On their bicycles, both young scientists simultaneously stopped to look back, as they parted.

Oh, yes, the conference party in the mountains of Tenerife was fantastic, but I suspect the reader is catching on (that conferences are not all-work-no-play affairs). I was honored to be a poster judge and tried to present the winners in quasi-English-Spanish doggerel. (Hey, Canary Islands, or Canarias, was named by the Romans, *Insulae Canariae*, or Islands of the Dogs.)

iii. Pepe Palacios. Pepe ran Tomás's lab and was probably assigned as my mentor. Pepe, Juan Imperial, and Tomás were *excellent* scientists. Pepe was also an outdoor type. I fondly remember hikes in the Sierra, canoeing, and combining culture and science with an outing. For instance, we took a commuter (*Cercanías*) train from Madrid to Las Zorreras (foxholes? foxy ladies?), the stop *before* El Escorial, so we could hike to this prodigious yet austere cathedral/mausoleum/monastery built during the reign of Philip II (1556-1592). Along the way, we skirted a well-fenced pasture of Miura bulls. Even from a distance, they inspired awe, gaining my new respect for toreadors. Along our trek, we had rewarding discussions on bacterial taxonomy and environmental microbiology.

Pepe was always "there," like meeting my mom at the airport (December 2000). She misread her ticket, confusing date of departure with date of arrival. Luckily that was the correct "incorrect" order, and she was not stranded at the airport on her *real* arrival the next morning. Mamma loved Spain, including

Pepe Palacios, El Escorial (coooold in December), Alicia's parents, and the market stalls of produce and seafood, a throwback to 86th Street. Surprisingly, she swooned over the tapas bars (*boquerones* were her favorite tapas: anchovies in vinegar, oil, and parsley) and their *bathrooms*. Not only had they beautiful fixtures and ceramics, but they were also very clean. Mamma especially loved that my three kids were visiting Spain that same Christmas 2000. My small apartment was beautifully chaotic.

In the intensely hot summer of 2003 I made a return visit to Madrid, and Pepe was the perfect host, taking me to the summer palace of the kings in Aranjuez (still very hot), and serving cool gazpacho at the home of his mom and dad, two very cool people. (Pepe mentioned that, in the old days, gazpacho was kept cool in a *fresquera* in a cubby in a very thick wall with a shaded northern exposure.) Dad was cool enough to urge me to use their shower, such a considerate gesture. Cool Mom was from the Alberti side—though I know nothing of any relation to poet of renown Rafael Alberti, and I have not asked.

iv. Manolo Pineda and his Rafi. Ahh, Manolo, my olive oil comrade, my window on the beautiful city of **Córdoba** (Federico García Lorca's *Lejana y Sola*); father of a family that extended from his beautiful home near this historic city's center to his lab at the University of Córdoba on its outskirts. I became a member of both families, and eventually Nancy joined us.

Early 2001, Manuel (Manolo) Pineda sent me a note in Madrid, inviting me to present a seminar in Córdoba on the assimilation of biologically fixed nitrogen in legumes. I knew of Manolo's work, but I did not know the man. He met me at the Córdoba train station of the high-speed AVE (*Alta Velocidad*

Córdoba is a marvelous city of history, architecture, and clashing cultures. One of its treasures, now lost, is my good buddy **Manolo Pineda,** here triumphantly showing off his winning Spanish tortilla, indeed a beauty, especially compared to my pathetic output which is hiding on my hard drive. (Rafi de Pineda: These are for you.)

Española). Several of his students showed me the highlights of this underappreciated city: Roman mosaics and columns, a huge mosque built over a Visigoth cathedral and in turn housing an imposing (in two ways) cathedral built by Carlos V, public baths that accommodated thousands during the Moorish reign, and a magnificent Roman bridge over the Guadalquivir, the river that brought New World loot up from Sevilla. That river still hosts rookeries of beautiful cattle egrets (*garzas ganaderas*) and glides past orange trees in fragrant bloom.

The city was enchanting and embracing, but that first evening when Manolo joined us, I was really hooked. Dr. Pineda was completely at home with his students, engaging in generous mutual ribbing and repartee. They seemed to respect him, and yet felt comfortable with him. Much later, when we called it a night, we came upon one of the "guilds" practicing steps for the Pasos de Cristo float procession for Easter Sunday two-plus months hence.

This could be a travelogue if I write too many details of encounters with Manolo and his Rafi, with whom Nancy later connected, and very much bonded. (Mary never met the Pinedas.) I would not flatter myself to call it a Washington Irving collection of stories, but one evening demonstrates the value that Spaniards put on friendship.

Jokes until 3 a.m. Nancy and I, sitting in Manolo and Rafi's kitchen for a nightcap, were exchanging jokes with our hosts. Funny how one joke dislodges the next, and so the evening went—we exchanged jokes until the wee hours. We wanted to leave. Our gracious hosts as well wanted to call it a long night. But I did not want to say, "OK, we're ready to go," because they were our hosts (and chauffeurs) and I did not want to appear to be a *mandón*, or pushy. Likewise, Manolo was inhibited for fear of appearing to be a terrible host. Somehow, the women communicated and off we went, Rafi and Nancy chuckling at their silly men. (And, I confess to falling prey to my machismo pride of having a bottomless pit of jokes.)

Manolo introduced me to at least three entrancing places in Andalucía. In 2010, I gave a talk in Benalauría—at an N-metabolism meeting (and exposed the assembled, including Nancy, to a poem in broken Spanish praising Spain). Benalauría had a reputation of harboring Moors who were "half-hearted" converts to Christianity after the fall of Granada. Ronda, also in Málaga, had magnificent settings—for example, an impressive bull ring and a bridge now in partial ruins that once traversed a huge, deep cavern.

The third locale was lovely cloud-borne Espejo, of white-washed humble buildings. Just outside Córdoba, it was Manolo's birthplace and the headquarters of the olive oil cooperative, Cooperativa Olivarera San Isidro. Manolo was its longtime and able president. On my first visit, we dropped in on his favorite producer, a prodigious lady, a *dueña*, whose home was full of artifacts of a bygone era, many to do with rearing horses (equine husbandry). But to me, her use of a Roman-era pillar to reinforce her front door frame was the pièce de résistance. (Which museum or monument could put it to better use?) She was the perfect hostess, offering conversation and wine, olives, bread, slices of manchego, jamón, and other wonders of charcuterie. In her life, she survived much, including the civil war, and when she passed a few years ago, she took with her a treasure trove of Spanish history.

I returned several times to Espejo, once taking part in the oil cooperative's annual board meeting, during which I was called upon to present an award. (Manolo, the rascal, sprang that on me *in momento*.)

Farewells. My life became intertwined with Spain and Spanish colleagues, even extending beyond the four families. Tomás and Carmina and Manolo have left us—even the most vivacious are susceptible to the passage of time and opportunistic pathogens.

Do not waste a single precious day.

My Friend Tomás
(1943–2020)

"Who might be this scientist of wide renown?"
Doctor Tomás—in his field, he wears a crown
Last name so Castilian: including the hyphen
"Ruiz-Argüeso," a star risen o'er his horizon

You accepted me, a stranger, into your group
Tomás, I joined your lab, not as part of a troop
Rather more a part of your close family nest
I felt both at home, and in science blest

Tomás, I was never your means to an award
I found my own in your heart's green sward
A pastoral refuge where our friendship flowered
With passion for science your humanity empowered

I came to love your Spain, Andalucía to León
With you and Carmina, I felt never alone
I became family in each ancestral home
A small part of your epic Iberian poem

But a malevolent destiny imposed its curse
Taking your Carmina, a fate most perverse
Then shortly thereafter, COVID in time
Called you away, Tomás, a doubly evil crime.

Yet, you did not leave, my kind, funny friend
As part of your large family, I try to extend
To bear witness to your goodness and love,
Strengths you embodied as David's dove

I feel your family's loving strong bond
In this era's darkness its good work lives on
Descendants extend your goodness enlightened
On your cultivated land, they thrive unfrightened

Yet another bittersweet farewell:

Manolo, My Man
(1952–2021)

Manolo, dear colleague and, yes, my friend
So approachable, with your quick rakish smile
Yet, with hearty skepticism you'd wend
A cudgel to my conclusions, but never to rile

For you, science was all about honesty
Data and theories trumped sensitive egos
Deferring to authority, yes was a travesty
Our "contra" dances were spirited fandangos

We came from such different places,
I, from a teeming Brooklyn casbah
You, from Humble Espejo's graces
Yet we buddies yell a holy ¡hurrah!

In "class" you showed loving forbearance
Teaching me to cook a Spanish tortilla
Would that I obliged in our kitchen dance,
'mano, you'da loved a Brooklyn pizzeria

Happily, Rafi and Nancy joined our duet
For maternal guidance, 'tis here confessed
They formed a bond, and never to forget
To keep us on the straight, narrow, and blessed

Manolo, I'm with you, Andalucian brother
We sit on the banks of the Guadalquivir
Sipping gin and tonic, kidding each other
Surveying domains, each a Moorish emir

Scratch an Italian, find a Spaniard. To my Spanish colleagues and friends: Nancy and I were exultant when Spain won the 2010 FIFA World Cup. We witnessed the final against Holland at an Athens (Greece) outdoor restaurant, with Dutch ladies at the next table. Their audible comments about how Holland dispatched Nancy's Uruguay in the semifinals were not appreciated. The ladies almost instigated a row. Peril was close at hand for they did not appreciate that they were outnumbered by Nancy.

*" I come from nowhere
Brooklyn, New York.
Williamsburg, Brooklyn.
These days Williamsburg
is kind of a hip area, but
when I grew up there,
the taxi drivers wouldn't
even go over the bridge, it
was so dangerous. "*

—Barry Manilow

Chapter Twenty-Three

• • •

BENSONHURST MAN IN ARGENTINA
(2005)

Over the last half of 2005, I took a Fulbright-sponsored teaching/research leave at the Argentine National University in Mar del Plata, a coastal city about 400 kilometers south of Buenos Aires. Mar del Plata blooms in the summer: Its beaches feature migrating whales, sea marathons, surfing, and fishing. The city is also the site of a major submarine base and has a thriving seafood industry. Its lovely bird sanctuary was pointed out to me by my visiting student, the peripatetic Erin Jarvis-Alberstat.

Nancy joined me in Argentina, and she took advantage of her stay to examine the school system, as well as to research African influences in Argentina and Uruguay. Mar del Plata is within easy reach of Montevideo, the Uruguayan capital across the Rio de la Plata by ferry (the "Boat-Bus") from Buenos Aires. Nancy has numerous relatives, good friends, and colleagues in Uruguay, including classmates of the University of the Republic School of Veterinary Medicine.

For me, taking a leave in Mar del Plata was all about science. Indeed, Argentina in general is renowned for its biosciences, having produced three Nobel laureates in medicine and biochemistry, though with 15 percent the population of the US and with a challenged infrastructure. I was very pleased to work with Professor Lorenzo Lamattina in his small but dynamically staffed laboratory. A year later, Lorenzo did a two-month stint in my Missouri lab; he was sponsored by a prestigious Guggenheim Foundation Fellowship.

(For the science-minded, Lorenzo has been a world leader in the generation and action of nitric oxide, NO, in plants. In animals, NO is a vasodilator, perhaps best known as the active

Celebration of a paper's acceptance. Nancy and Joe on the flanks, Lorenzo third from Joe. Goodies from a local *Salumeria/Latticini Freschi*. Food is Italian, drink is Scotch. I'd have loved to have this group in my lab.

derivative of nitroglycerin administered to victims of angina. NO also plays a role in the action of *Viagra*™.)

There is an old saw about Argentinians who will enter a revolving door behind you and exit in front of you. I did find them exceptionally resourceful, and their students very well trained— they are prized by top labs in Europe and the US. More than one American colleague told me that when a piece of equipment is "on the fritz," the American student will usually "call in" technical support or a replacement, while the Argentinian will fix it or figure out a work-around.

Lorenzo's lab prepared sterile growth media in used Gatorade jars in autoclaves that were tantamount to oversized pressure cookers. Small tools to be sterilized were wrapped in newspaper in those pressure cookers. And the personnel worked well together, contrary to the stereotype of the cranky, pushy Argentine: There was one sterile transfer hood in my five-story building, and all hewed to a strict schedule of use, each user leaving it clean for the next.

Personally, my interactions with faculty, staff, students, and Argentines in general ranged from "wonderful" to "interesting." This covers the gamut of *El Argentino*, loved, or loathed by much of the rest of Latin America. I believe that serious economic blows have made Argentines more human in the eyes of their continental compadres. I believe, also, that Argentines no longer see themselves as quite so exceptional. Then again, I'm used to having my beliefs shattered, especially in light of their FIFA 2022 Cup championship.

My Argentinian move was more radical than sabbatical leaves in Massachusetts or Spain. A radical change of venue is akin to going through "growing pains" yet again, stepping back from man to boy. I recommend this "re-coming of age" in order to stay humble, to broaden narrowed perspectives, and to live new daily challenges. When you go out on the streets "you never know." Being a pedestrian in Bensonhurst of the '50s and '60s sharpened my instincts for crossing the streets of Mar del Plata in 2005.

Overall, I experienced a broad view of Argentina, a country that I hope is not receding from realizing its prodigious potential. I hope, also, that the same will not be said of the USA, so hamstrung are we by political division and racism. Argentina, like the US, is a country of immigrants and a checkered history of dealing with indigenous peoples. Salvatore La Puma, Professor Lamattina, and I are part of the Italian diaspora. (I put myself in good company, no?) Lorenzo told me that his post-WWII family migrated to both Americas. (I note there is a LaMattina Foundation in NYC, which funds zoological conservation work.) Argentina, like the US, has benefited from the immigrant influx. Pardon the understatement.

Lows and Highs of My Argentine Experience

Low 1: Welcome to the way we are. I had been in Argentina before, both as a tourist and as a participant at a conference where I first met Lorenzo. This time I came to teach and to do lab work. I carried a small piece of equipment to hand over to a faculty member at my host institution in Mar del Plata. It was purchased by a scientist at the University of Colorado. He and his Argentine colleague were co-investigators on a grant that paid for the device. I was armed with a letter of explanation, and other papers.

At Customs, a very good-looking young man in sparkling clean and trim uniform asked about the item. After inspecting it and going over the papers, he asked me to step into a small room which, to me, appeared to be a repository for seized items.

"Give me $100."

"Is this an import fee?" I replied as I handed over a 100-dollar bill. I got no answer.

"Do I get a receipt?" I asked with little hope because by this time I knew I had paid a bribe (a *mordida,* or bite, in Mexico, a *coima* in Argentina).

He stamped the box, as I recall, and returned it. I was met by Nancy and Lorenzo and explained what just happened.

"Sorry you had to see what happens in this country," said Lorenzo. He followed with a promise that I would be reimbursed. I repeated this story several times, certainly to the item's recipient—a very cordial and competent lady, and a driven scientist. Everyone commiserated. I mourned the blatant corruption more than never being reimbursed. But I was not overly bitter. In La Puma's Bensonhurst and mine, only *schlemiels* and *chooches* never get a piece of the pie.

Low 2. *Cascarrabias/Gruñones.* I love these terms that are almost onomatopoetic for crotchety old men. I don't mean to paint Argentina as full of cantankerous crusty curmudgeons. We interacted with many charming elderly folks, and at the other end of the age spectrum my interaction with students was a joy (*infra vide*). But one incident brought home this "geriatric" trait that I saw more than once outside the university.

Nancy and I were waiting in line at the Mar del Plata main post office to ship some soybeans to my collaborator in Porto Alegre, Brazil. When the elderly guy in front of us finally made it to the window, he got increasingly frustrated with postal regulations. His interaction with the postal official became increasingly acrimonious until, finally, one last regulation and/or form was all the elderly postal patron could take—he left, fuming.

The official seemed overjoyed to see him go. I stepped up to the window with Nancy. She was all smiles and greeted the official in her best rioplatense (the "dialect" of Uruguay and Argentina). Things were going swimmingly until he asked about the package contents. Like a *tarado* (rioplatense for "nincompoop"), I replied, "soybeans" which required phytosanitary certificates and so on. I knew at least not to say *mutant* soybeans. (And, dear reader, they were greenhouse raised and were *not* GMO.) The official was deflated, but Nancy interjected "*maquillaje,*" or "cosmetics." He gladly put that on the postal form, and off we went. There are times when lies promote peace.

I have seen this scenario played out, in different dialect, at my Benson Avenue Brooklyn Post Office branch (11214), where I always try to be civil and agreeable. The branch is a block up from the St. Finbar parish where Mario's wife confessed too much and too frequently to Father Hartigan (*Gravesend Bay [1940]*), and where Vito Conti stole the altar's gold monstrance, "a sunburst on a stem" (*The Boys of Bensonhurst [1942]*). One night in my middle age, the bronze downspouts of the parish's rain gutters were ripped off. I'm sure that was not the only affront St. Finbar endured. By the way, its beloved parish priest was the child of a Jewish-Italian marriage, pure Bensonhurst roots. He was *not* a grouchy old man. Take heed, Argentina.

Low 3. Visa renewal. Fulbright approved my stay for five months, but Argentina insisted on granting me a renewable three-month visa. This necessitated a visit to an immigration office mostly frequented by poor folks from Bolivia, Paraguay, and other places with a high percentage of indigenous people. This was the southern cone equivalent of the USA's southern border, across which come folks seeking employment in factories, fields, slaughterhouses, etc. I detected a definite disrespect by Argentinian officials for these folks—for example, addressing them in the familiar. (Oh, and contrary to Argentines' European self-image, there is a high percentage of indigenous DNA sequences in the national genome.)

Low to High 4. The communal lunch. If Argentines did not score points with me in the immigration office, at times I failed to uphold the best image of the USA at the National University of Mar del Plata.

I usually took my lunch in the library reading/seminar room of the university's Institute of Biological Research, a setting that gave folks a chance to see me up close, and eventually to talk frankly of the USA and of Argentina. Hurricane Katrina devastated New Orleans during the first third of our stay. Nancy loves New Orleans and felt the disaster in a personal way. University folks mentioned how seemingly inadequate our response was in coming to the aid of victims, the *damnificados* (and most of them Black). I should have thought before explaining the confusion as "New Orleans is the most Latino of American cities" which, even if taken in the best light, was not flattering to my hosts.

My colleagues noted the large number of Black folks seeking refuge in the Houston Astrodome (the scene was indeed a horror), to which I commented, "Well, at least they have cars to get there."

My mouth needed a safety latch. Upon both of those utterances, I felt like crawling into my lunch bag. We eventually all agreed that President George W. Bush was not prepared for the disaster, and that we *americanos* should have handled the situation much better. And I totally agreed that the disaster pulled back the covers on some ugly racism. My colleagues took my enlightened and educated outlook as sincere.

Overall, my lunchroom highs outweighed the lows.

Low 5. The Triennial Summit of the Americas. My experiences on campus and in town usually qualified as a high. One possible exception was that Mar del Plata hosted the triennial Summit of the Americas, attended in 2005 by George W. Bush. It was headquartered across from our apartment. Nancy and I left town to avoid "quarantine" and ruckus. For ruckus, two examples:

i. A women's activist group chanted, seemingly for hours: "*Bush, fascista, vos sos el terrorista.*" (Fascist Bush, *you* are the terrorist.)

ii. Neighborhood riots and vandalism were transmitted to our hotel TV in Brazil where we had escaped for a short visit.

While university people did not suspect I had anything to do with the summit, I learned that some of the folks in our neighborhood gym thought I was doing advance work for it. I think I convinced them otherwise. Most of them, anyway.

High 1. Relationships with townsfolk. We lived on the 14th floor of one of the tallest buildings (of about 25 floors) in town. Our apartment terrace looked out on the beach. A wine shop next door offered the Norton brand of an excellent Argentine Malbec, for a mere three pesos (at the time, a little over a dollar a bottle). On the way home from the university to my apartment, I interacted with street folks plying their trades—hawking newspapers, lottery tickets, fresh jelly palm fruit, etc.—86th Street in Rioplatense. Before entering the elevator, I'd stop and chat with building personnel who commented on events at the national and local government levels. Of course, I was expected to reciprocate with my own commentary on American domestic and foreign policy.

Our *verdulero* (greengrocer) greeted me every morning as I walked past his stand to my bus.

"*Buendía, José querido.*"

"*Buenos días, Carlos.*"

I loved that Carlos addressed me as "dear." He had lots of questions about the US, including American baseball. (The 2005 World Series was broadcast on the Argentinian affiliate of ESPN.) He was full of recipes, and his constant advice was that when something is taken out of the oven it keeps on cooking, *sigue cocinando*, until the interior cools. Nancy and I still use this phrase, more than seventeen years later.

Across the street, our laundry/dry cleaning guy (*tintorero*) was a font of political observations and commentary on the Argentine reality. I learned from him that an Argentine (Dr. René Favaloro—sounds like an immigrant, no?) performed the first coronary bypass surgery. He also claimed that the pioneering doctor eventually committed suicide, so ungrateful was Argentine society for his accomplishment. (Suicide is the going theory of his demise: https://www.theguardian.com/news/2000/aug/03/guardianobituaries.)

Once, while the *tintorero* was in the back looking for our order, a customer came in and started recounting moments in Argentine football history, just as I would have done about the old days of the Brooklyn Dodgers back in La Puma's Bensonhurst.

From the back: "Eduardo, you're talking to an American; he doesn't know much about our football." I got an apologetic look from Eduardo.

"Don't worry, Eduardo. I feel the same way about Brooklyn baseball."

We had access to excellent Italian-style cheeses and salumeria (cured pork products), as well as to fresh seafood (and to the sea, a mere three blocks away). A seafood shop proprietor prominently displayed a picture of his boyhood home on the Bay of Naples. He got teary-eyed when I told him my mother's side was from the same area. His seafood was excellent—each day a new daily catch—and I got a great lesson on cleaning squid.

High 2. El Zafarrancho. Nancy and I disagree on the meaning of the nautical term, *zafarrancho*, either a "big mess" (says Nancy), or its cleanup, "clearing the decks," appropriate for a town with a naval base and a vibrant fishing industry. (We're both right according to my dictionaries.) But the important point for this discussion is that El Zafarrancho was a wonderful (and wonderfully immaculate) neighborhood restaurant. Our "regular" waitress was a sincere young lady, a jewel. We managed to get her to sit for a picture with Nancy's visiting journalist friend, Tracy Barnett (editor of the University of Missouri Journalism School's *Adelante*). Tracy and Nancy then went off for a week exploring the indigenous cultures and natural beauty of Salta, a northern province in the Andes. I had to stay behind to teach. Life is full of trade-offs. I made the effort that Nancy did not have to deal with an apartment *zafarrancho*, in either of its meanings, upon her return from Salta.

High 3. The Institute of Biological Research annual picnic and football match. The weather and our relations with Argentines warmed as we approached December's southern cone summer. It was the month of our institute picnic/barbecue, featuring the Argentine dual passion for soccer and for beef barbecued over glowing wood embers. The ferocious soccer match produced only a couple of serious injuries, but also induced a serious collective appetite. Lorenzo was the chief *asador* (barbecue master) and kept the ravenous horde at bay with heavenly *choripan* (either a beef sausage [*chorizo*] or a blood sausage [*morcilla*] on hearty Italian bread) until the real cuts were ready. Finally, when all were seated and sated, I read an ode of thanks to my hosts. The following is a shorter version of a multi-limerick ode. (The original was in Spanish and I liked it better. I wrote it when I was steeped in rioplatense.)

Asado (or Roast—English for a loving spoof)

Friends, I have learned that the Argentine is brave
To face strikes and protests, and futbol rage
    and that in every car
    from Jujuy to Pinamar
Is a driver of courage on hell's highways

"Get in, hold on, sit down and shut up"
A warning with which passengers put up
    saith the sign on my bus
    that I heed without fuss
I see now why y'all chug yerba by the cup

Which inspires, my hosts, this literary toast
From Mafalda to Borges* you are the utmost
    so, to you, an olé!
    and well-done che!
And know that my ode is not verbal compost

Kidding you not, indeed you all accepted me
Though I was locked in a zone not quite free
      in Bush's secure area
      as if I carried malaria
You invited me, not GWB, to this grand partee

And thank you, Lorenzo, for all you have done
From invitation to reception, is a long run
      you covered every base
      at a magnificent pace
Which to me means that you hit a homerun

* *Mafalda to Borges*: Mafalda is a comic strip little girl of great wisdom and pithy sayings. Jorge Luis Borges was a genius Argentinian writer/essayist.

High 4. Teaching was a joy (and always is when the students are motivated). Part of my duties was to teach a graduate-level course, which was a trip—the students were so motivated and prepared. (Who ever heard of the *Ugly American*?) In "Genetic Tools in Plant Physiology," I tried to introduce each new topic with a rhyme—obviously a character defect on my part. For the last class, before we repaired to happy hour, the graduate students regaled me with their own image-laden poetry.

I included a representative student poem in my bilingual poetry volume, *A Life's Rambles/Ramblas de una Vida*. Victoria María Martín (Vicky) was the poet. During the preparation of my "poetic" compilation, Vicky and I reconnected, seventeen years after my departure. She is doing well, productive in science with a permanent position, and in family matters with two kids.

Speaking of talented students, American research labs lost many opportunities to take in Argentinians. 9/11 made it difficult for students to acquire US visas, but many Mar del Plata students were dual citizens—Italian/Argentinian, Spanish/Argentinian, etc.—so the EU countries were their "oyster." Entry into one gave unimpeded access to the pearls of the others. (Sorry, UK.)

Nancy and I lived near the palatial Italian consulate in Mar del Plata. We could have dropped in to initiate paperwork to become dual Italian/American citizens, but we did not bother.

High 5. We saw more of Argentina than we had bargained for. Shaking the rafters of my memory attic, I am amazed at how much we stuffed into five months—youth helps. Nancy and I attended a national biochemistry conference in Córdoba, where we connected with my former postdoctoral associate, Ariel Goldraij, a successful professor at the National University in Córdoba. We enjoyed the town—Córdoba was named a UNESCO Heritage Site for its Spanish colonial architecture. It was indeed lovely, as were the green surroundings.

But then we saw more. Argentina hit us with a reality blow: during the conference, Aerolíneas Argentinas went on strike. We were obliged to ride a bus twenty hours back to Mar del Plata. A highlight was the driver's assistant periodically moving up the aisle with a tray of whiskey shots, which almost made up for disgruntled airline strikers trying to block traffic.

This was not exactly a "high," but it was a great cultural excursion.

La Rioja is not the Rioja wine region of Spain. It is the capital of the remote and dry province of La Rioja. I accepted an invitation to its national university to meet the expectation that I network with Fulbright scholars, past or present. I gave two research talks, a radio interview, and a class on bioethics, of all things. I was impressed, as always, with the intellectual level and maturity of the students, especially the all-female ethics class that discussed issues from abortion to gender equality. Men would have benefitted had they enrolled.

While in the region, Nancy and I went to the wilds of the Andean foothills, visiting a national park full of geological formations ("Grand Canyon Lite") and tough *algarrobo* trees— source of the famous carob chocolate substitute. If La Rioja is remote, the twin Provincial Park, Talampaya/Ischigualasto (Valle de la Luna) in the "rain shadow" of the Andes, is almost lunar.

Two young men from a travel agency drove us from La Rioja to the parks and back, and we almost ran out of gas in the vast arid wasteland. We convinced them to turn off the AC to improve our gas mileage. I have a strong memory of these two fine young fellows refusing a tip. Indeed, their gratuity was our gratitude for their great conversation and insight into Argentina.

How different were they from that young customs agent I met upon my arrival.

Chapter Twenty-Four

• • •

BENSONHURST MAN BACK IN BENSONHURST
(2012–2013)

Angelo's 20th Avenue barbershop. Over 2012 and 2013, I spent parts of fourteen consecutive months back in the 'hood: Mamma was fighting a losing battle against recurrent breast cancer. This vignette is about Mamma, but also about how neighborhoods as well reach the end of a life stage. "Die" is too strong, but they certainly metamorphose. Being a transient inhabitant of Bensonhurst reinforced to me the truism that you can go back, but you can't go back to the way it used to be. I was not in my Bensonhurst of the 1950s and '60s, and certainly not in the 'hood about 75 years before 2013, years so well-painted by La Puma, years when magical realism and the evil eye were much more prominent.

I needed a haircut and I was far from my Mizzou Campus Barbershop. There were two shops near Mamma's apartment, both on busy 20th Avenue. One was an ornate unisex spot, with metallic turban hairdryers, white-smocked hairdressers, and a *mui gavarim pa-ruuski* ("we speak Russian") sign inside the front picture window. To me, way too fancy and, I admit, too Russian—certainly not of the 'hood of my youth. Angelo's barbershop was on 75th Street just across 20th Avenue from Mamma's St. Dominic RC Church (with its special shrine to Padre Pio of Pietralcina). Angelo's looked much more inviting than the Russian place, and I would bet Angelo was Sicilian.

The establishment had three chairs and one barber, Angelo at your service. The facade was like my stepfather's storefront three decades earlier—large wood-framed glass panes on one side of a recessed door—no attempt at glitz or remodeling. Angelo was very functional. He also had a kiddy chair, and a TV that transmitted only Rai Uno, the major Italian public station.

On a Friday evening, I popped my head in and asked a virile-looking, stocky, middle-aged Angelo, thick hairy forearms sticking out of his white smock, if he was open on Saturday. He nodded a "yes." The next day, a young guy was in "the chair" and two older guys were in the "audience" seats. Think of the barbershop in Eddie Murphy's *Coming to America* (John Landis, director, 1988) except that nobody was African American, and the only barber was Angelo. No one was watching an Italian cartoon show on Rai Uno. One of the audience guys was chatting with Angelo in Italian. The other was reading the *New York Times*, in English, of course. When the young guy's haircut was finished, he chatted amiably with Angelo, in Italian, while paying up. The other Italian speaker took his place in the chair while, from his audience seat, the New York Times guy made some comments to Angelo, in Italian.

Mannaggia! Do you have to speak Italian to get a haircut here?

Mr. New York Times' haircut was finished, my turn. I sat in the chair with some trepidation saying my mentally rehearsed, "*Non parlo niente d'italiano*" (I don't speak any Italian), to which Mr.

New York Times and a new patron laughed. Angelo, sonuvagun, refused to speak anything *but* Italian. Somehow, I got across that I wanted a full head buzz, "*la macchina al numero due, sopra tutta la testa*" (the clippers at the 2 mm setting, all over.) Overall, I experienced a cultural excursion to the way things used to be in the neighborhood.

I couldn't wait to get back to Mamma's apartment to relay the story. When I left for the barber, Mamma Vina was alone. On my return, five "cousins" were visiting—it was raucous, as it should have been. Mamma loved the company. She was everyone's Aunt Vina, making me everyone's cousin. I am sure that her extended family helped keep her alive.

I got a wonderful dose of Bensonhurst that day, the way it was, kind of. Did Sal La Puma work through Padre Pio to make Angelo's an Italian hot spot?

My return to Bensonhurst and my ailing Mamma evoked memories, and not just of Sunday sauce, homegrown basil, or goo-gootz. (Pardon the repetition: goo-gootz = green calabash = cucuzza—crunchier than zucchini, great in a primavera sauce over rigatoni.)

The Bensonhurst I knew was dying, as was Mamma. Is this a way to become a man, with no hope of going back to boyhood?

My Bensonhurst—Gnarly, Enveloping Womb

In a stew pot's multi-scented minestrone
And on a numbing cold knife-edge
Hot humid anger and icy streets I've known
So, *goombah/landsman* don't drive a wedge

221

We both sprouted from this cold concrete
Along with *basilicó* and gravid goo-gootz
Though our hard eyes don't dare to meet
We're green shoots from the same gnarly roots

Our County of Kings, Borough of Churches
Is our defining anchor, our "spirit of place"
Though my wandering ship tosses and lurches
I dock in Bensonhurst's primal embrace

My Bensonhurst, your dialect may change
Your minestrone, with new ingredients mixed
Your transformations can never derange
My moorings, now ever more firmly fixed

Bensonhurst, you helped me face it all
Your blows have imbued me with strength
I journey ever back to your mercurial thrall
Your constant change has my changeless consent

I returned to the old neighborhood, four years later—to give my *Vina* memoir book talk at the iconic Spumoni Gardens (86th Street and 27th Avenue). Back on 20th Avenue, Angelo was still in his place and in his barber's tunic, but this time he was chatting with a woman and a youngster, apparently her son and Angelo's customer. Paint was peeling on the sign over the establishment, and there was a notice on cardboard taped inside the window: "Barbershop for Sale."

I wanted to drop in to say hello but did not want to interrupt. I still kick myself for not going in. A true Bensonhurst man would have.

But later that same day, I dropped in at the 20th Avenue and 78th Street Mondiale Bakery. And there she was, Donna Carmina, still tending to customers from behind the counter. Periodically, she yelled in Sicilian dialect to her husband in the backroom stromboli of ovens and who knows what else? La Donna remembered Mamma, from four-plus years before. I learned from a conversation she had with two patrons that she picked up some Spanish. "And where did you learn Spanish?" I asked her, in Spanish, *naturalmente.*

"From-a de televizh."

Bensonhurst always changes, and in this important way it's always the same. And as always, the semolina bread and cannoli were great.

In the early 1970s, in back of our store, Mrs. Lucia (Lucy) Spadaro had just passed a polaroid of her new grandbaby to Mamma. Lucy was expunged for the 2016 book cover (right bottom). That Photoshop travesty is herewith corrected. Mr. Spadaro would water my meager tomato and bietola (swiss chard) plants through the fence, before the yard was paved over. He tapped into subsurface water and his hand-operated water pump got both yards through low-water years.

Chapter Twenty-Five

• • •

MOTHERS ARE IN BENSONHURST, AND EVERYWHERE

(forever)

> Your Bensonhurst and mine, Mr. La Puma,
> is a breeding pond where neighborhood fry
> can develop to a priest or to a wise guy,
> amid mothers' prayers for *Buona Fortuna*

As a retired professor of biochemistry, going on sixteen years of emeritus status, I'm about to step into Dante's ring of vanishing scientific importance. I do not fret. Science is now most important to me because of the relationships born of collaboration, teaching, and travel.

Beyond science, or within, what better relationship than that of a mother and her children?

Peruvian Mother's Day, 1973. Right out of graduate school, our young family moved to Cali, Colombia. More than a year into our stay, we took a family vacation flying to Lima, Peru, with two kids, one-year-old Joseph and three-year-old Laura. We arranged no lodging or itinerary. It *was* the Age of Aquarius. But we were nevertheless well-equipped with the history and traditions of the Inca and other pre-Columbian cultures. We knew what we wanted to see and experience.

Well-equipped or not, we bore the aspects of a couple just off the VW bus from Woodstock. I had a full beard and unruly hair, contrasting with my wife, Mary—a gorgeous blue-eyed auburn-blonde in shape-revealing bellbottoms. People thought I was Cuban, while they usually just stared at Mary. Upon landing in Lima, a *taxista* informed us we were out of luck—all hotels were full. He made a tour of *pensiones* and boardinghouses, some quite humble. No vacancies, no luck. Two young children in tow did not help our cause. Finally, we met a lady who ran a *pensión* in her converted fourth-floor apartment. It was reached by walking through a bookstore to her courtyard access.

The lady personified a middle-aged, short, stocky mother-in-law. She looked at baby Joseph, and then turned to me. "He cries, no? My walls are thin."

"He's a quiet baby, very calm (*muy tranquilo*)." I lied.

Probably reading our desperation, the lady relented. Certainly, Joseph's large expressive dark eyes and Laura's blue and green eye combination and tired countenance had nothing to do with her decision. Importantly, we had a room. We admonished young Joseph not to wake the snoring bear on the other side of a flimsy divider that did not even make it to the ceiling.

While in Lima we often arrived at our *pensión* after bookstore hours. The books, nestled behind iron grating and protective glass, lined a passageway of wisdom, history, and learning, accompanying us to our welcoming, humble lodging.

We had a wonderful time in Lima, and long side trips to Machu Picchu, Titicaca, Sacsayhuaman, Cuzco, Puna, and the rugged, stark *altiplano* high plain. Indigenous women got a kick out of a *gringo* dad carrying a baby on his back, Incan style. I was an honorary Mamá. Little Joseph was a conversation starter, though we had a scare in Macchu Picchu when he tried to crawl out of his carrier to look over my shoulder for a better view down the Sacred Valley, thousands of feet deep.

Returning to Lima from our forays meant returning to our landlady/mother-in-law who was becoming comfortable with us. We got to know her family, well enough even for frank talk about politics.

When it was time to fly back to Cali, landlady arranged for her taxi-driver brother to pick us up at four a.m. for the trip to the Lima airport. In the chill and darkness of a humble Lima *barrio*, brother *taxista* showed up at the appointed hour. So did his sister—*la señora* came downstairs in her housecoat. She *had* to say goodbye to Laura, and especially to Little Joseph, whom she hugged and kissed. Then, sobbing, she wished us all *feliz viaje*, a safe and happy trip back to Cali.

Motherhood, you know no nationality.

Mother's Day Eve, 2018. I was excited about a going-away party at the Columbia, Missouri, apartment of a visiting Brazilian scholar. I originally met Claudete Santa-Catarina in 2005, during my Argentine sabbatical when we initiated a collaboration. So, this Mother's Day was the juxtaposition of motherhood, collegiality, and Latin America.

Claudete, as a mother of two, called herself *uma mãe coruja*, literally a mother owl, a fierce but loving mom. She and her nestling owlets recall my own mamma whose dark, wide-eyed visage was owl-like to many. Mamma's eyes radiated love, but also took in potential signals of danger.

Claudete and scientist husband, Vanildo, were royal hosts. Among other delights, they served *feijoada*, or "big bean dish." As for so many iconic dishes, *feijoada* was born of poverty and hunger (*'a misèria* in Neapolitan dialect). Brazilian slave owners ate the best cuts "high on the hog," and the slaves did the best they could with knuckles, hog jowls, pig's feet, and what we today romanticize as chitterlings—bluntly offal, or internal organs and intestines. It all went into a large pot with those lovely black beans and a few bitter greens. Nowadays, the best Brazilian restaurants serve *feijoada*. The cuts are higher, though, and chitlins are banished.

Feijoada is a mother's loving care borne of humble raw materials.

I received an April 2021 email from Claudete: "Now we are five, André was born on May 5, 2020 . . . now almost one year." He was an unexpected COVID baby and is beautiful, and is being watched over by owl eyes.

Italian Mother's Day. My mamma's Sunday *ragú*, or meat sauce, had meatballs, of course. At times, it also had a cultural connection to *'a misèria* of the old days—a porcine tribute, body parts we called *cútuna*, literally, the *skin* of hooves, ears, etc. After simmering three to five hours the *cútuna* and the tomato sauce melded into a lovely fusion. That sauce tormented us with its primeval aroma from mid-Sunday morning to our afternoon repast. Ragú from a supermarket shelf? My immigrant Nonna,

Grandma Nunziatina, would retort *"Ma quando? MAI!!"* But when? NEVER!!

In Bensonhurst, we learned to appreciate that every Sunday was Mother's Day. It was real, and so was Mamma's (and Nonna's) cooking. As I walked down Bay 31st Street late Sunday mornings looking for stickball buddies, the aromas wafting out of the homes were both authentic and auto-identifying, like fingerprints. The homes all had them, but they uniquely "fingered" the bearer, la mamma.

Mr. La Puma could say the above better than I just did, no doubt. For me, such a stroll evokes Sal La Puma's stories, about deaf mothers (*The Mouthpiece [1940]*) who dealt with the world through a hearing son, about a gangster's widow who fell in love with a wise guy who almost got her son killed on a heist (*The Gangster's Ghost [1939]*), about a Jewish mother . . . I'll say no more, Sal is squirming, and I ain't no rat.

Morgan's Mom. In putting this retrospective together, I have reconnected with Morgan, stirring my memory about her strong and caring mom, Jane. I was captivated by Morgan, sure, but her mom also had me in thrall, and I felt obliged to live up to her standards of good taste and behavior.

Jane died in 2004 "after a long and interesting life." I'll say. She was born in China to two M.D.s. She was trained in art at Oberlin and the University of New Mexico, and was well-positioned to help foster the racial integration of civic groups in Southern Maryland's Calvert County. In those groups, she practiced, or applied, her art, therefore extending it to the human level. Her great interest in people and "lively curiosity" was probably the result of her early exposure to other cultures as a global nomad. So, in Maryland she was not only a dedicated Mom, she was happy to "settle in" after years of moving around as a child and young person.

Mother Jane gave Morgan and me "space," which I very much appreciated. Yet, when I exhibited a bout or two of bad judgment (yes, even me), she spoke to me sternly, in private. She appealed to my sense of "what is right," in no way pulling rank.

Jane and Vina would have been the best of buddies—the perfect pairing of moms with two sons or two daughters. And, I know that Jane would never lord over Vina her creds in higher education or training. Indeed, I'd have loved to see their collaboration on artistic projects that involved fabrics or other media.

Mothers in my Life. This reminiscence covers the transitions from my mother Vina, my wife Mary, to my life partner Nancy. Nancy and Mary are each a mother of three (Nancy's by her late husband who passed when she was pregnant with her third.)

My mother, Vina, was a woman of strength and unselfish love. She raised my brother and me, at times under extreme conditions, times when she was a single mom, like her own mother, my Nonna, Nunziatina. Vina was a loving mother-in-law as well to my wife Mary. Mary and I have three kids who benefited both from their grandmother ("Noni" Vina) and Mary who will always be an excellent, loving mom. Our three kids are people of accomplishment: Two are Phi Beta Kappa and the third is no slouch, but I brag no more, lest I invoke the evil eye *malocchio* that still haunts this Bensonhurst boy, almost as much as it haunted my Mamma Vina and Grandma, Nonna Nunziatina.

I had a good life with Mary as we took on the challenge of managing three kids and two careers in two continents. We also dealt with the challenge of Mary's gender discrimination suit against our Department of Biochemistry and the University of Missouri, the whole long process initiated with a labor grievance during our sabbatical year in Massachusetts (1989–1990). I admire Mary's tenacity, her willingness to push back at adversity, her sense of adventure. Our three kids benefited from her open-mindedness to the extent that they are as "nonracist" and accepting of others as I could ever have hoped.

Mary eventually separated from the MU Biochemistry Department in which her association was fraught with internalized feelings that some viewed her as an unwelcomed "spousal accommodation." Those are deadly words in academia, and the spouse almost always is the wife.

Our split up is an all-too-common example of a couple, with children, seeking individual advancement in an academic environment, especially in a market in which there is virtually one major league in town. (Albeit a large and varied one. Mizzou is near the top quartile of American class I research universities and among the best in plant sciences.) The biochemistry department was a complicated milieu for us, one in which it was difficult to carve out two independent programs. But what speaks to Mary's quality, intellect, and fortitude is that she became well-ensconced in a new permanent position in the USDA unit at MU, and in a fundamentally different discipline—maize genomics. Mary handled such radical changes with forbearance, strength and collegiality. She was very good at her new field and so recognized by the maize genetics community at large, becoming curator of the Maize Genome Database (Maize DB).

Nancy, a mother of three, a lady of accomplishment, is a very involved grandma, a *nana*. She came to the US as a widow, on a United Nations fellowship, to pursue a Masters in animal reproductive biology, to go along with her DVM degree in large animal medicine. (If she could handle bulls and horses, and three rambunctious kids, there was no hope for me.) She now is an interpreter and teaches Spanish in various settings.

Life moves on, and it has treated all of us well, except for the slings and arrows of creeping old age. There is a Neapolitan expression, here in "correct" Tuscan dialect:

La vecchiaia è una carogna, ma per chi non ci arriva è una vergogna. (A shame if you don't get to experience rotten old age.)

Mamma was ever ready to be a mom, nonna, and mother-in-law. With grandson, Joseph, in her Bensonhurst apartment, 2006. (He was in New York visiting his fiancée, Linda Kim, who was getting her Nursing degree at NYU.) Linda and Joseph have 10-year-old Luca Jun.

Chapter Twenty-Six

• • •

FOUR OLD MEN ON AN ISLAND OFF MAINE

(July 2022)

Four old men on an island off Maine
We sit, sip, rock, and reminisce
On misadventures, our common refrain:
Without mistakes—life would be remiss

Too old to resurrect the old-time spunk
That almost sent us to an early Hades
By life's sweet blows we're now punch-drunk
By lefts and rights from our loving ladies

We four old guys on Chebeague Island—Sam Gaskins, Bob Hudak, Joe, and now introducing Dave Carey—are not only survivors but successful in our fields, though Joe hopes his career has not careened out of control by lane shifting from science to writing. We four have lived a combined 220-plus years since our Cornell graduations. A glance at the actuarial tables tells me we have a lot to be thankful for, and much of that thanks goes to the women in our lives, with whom we have been associated/married for more than two hundred of those years.

Though we mercilessly kidded each other about our college and postgraduate love lives, our "missed opportunities," we all ended up with women of accomplishment, women strong in their careers, achievers, nurturers, women with open minds who earned advanced degrees while keeping their families together. Indeed, our women, and our *mothers*, are undoubtedly the reason we made it this far, able to meet at Juniper Lodge on Chebeague Island.

So, let's get to the women in our lives, already.

Sam's Testimonial. "My maternal grandmother, Psyche Ceres Hadcock, and her sister-in-law, Aunt Bea, founded Juniper Lodge. The two ladies along with my grandmother's three daughters, Editha, Ceres (my mother), and Thora, ran it as a tourist lodge (max capacity ca. 35) from 1914 to 1940. Today, it is still only accessible from the mainland by ferry, water taxi, or barge. WWII closed down the Portland/Casco Bay harbor and essentially ended tourism. After the war, the lodge became a family summer camp with a capacity of around twenty."

Joe's Two Cents. They established the lodge six years before the 1920 ratification of the 19th Amendment that guaranteed (white) women's voting rights, after way too long a struggle. At first, the lodge was not appointed with internal plumbing nor with electricity. Heating was by fireplace and woodstoves. In 2022, we were spoiled: The main house had all the amenities, and we three visiting males were lodged in individual peripheral cabins that had electricity thanks to Sam's electrical engineer dad, Darius. The surrounding woods were for nocturnal exercises in plant water relations and nitrogen metabolism. Bathrooms in the main house were available to all of us, as was morning coffee and breakfast. The screened-in dining room offered magnificent views of other islands and the mainland, as we tore into lobsters and each other's reminiscences.

Sam's Testimonial, continued. "The two large pictures over the piano were of my grandmother's parents, Ezra Heywood and his wife, Angela Tilton Heywood, my great-grandparents. Together they published *The Word: A Monthly Journal of Reform*, which was thought to be an anarchist's magazine, and so judged as obscene. It supported women's suffrage, birth control, free love, and free speech. Ezra was jailed in 1878 for violating the 1873 Comstock Act (the "Chastity Laws"). Angela was considered the driving force behind the publication, but Ezra took the fall. Both can be googled. Their daughter, Psyche Ceres Heywood, my grandmother, married twice, first to Edward Hadcock and later Henry Bradshaw.

"My grandmother, her three daughters and their half-brother, Daniel Bradshaw, lived in Boston fall through spring. It was there they boarded my father, Darius, while he attended MIT. My mother, Ceres Hadcock, told her two sisters 'he's mine' and it was a done deal. Their 1932 marriage lasted sixty-two years."

Joe's Two Cents, with interest. Recall that before that ill-considered 1964 hike from Falls Church, Virginia, to Miami, Florida, Sam's mom, Ceres, ordered me to "take care of Kelly," my fellow hitchhiker (Chapter Eleven). Ms. Ceres commanded respect.

I point out Ceres's "He's mine" comment. Sam asserted that in spite of us guys claiming to be aggressive suitors, we actually got bagged by women who chose *us*. As I think back, Sam might be right.

Dave Carey's Testimonial to "His" Women. "I first met Charlene when I double-dated with Sam at a Baltimore Janis Joplin concert. I told Sam that night that I was going to marry her."

Joe's Two Cents, with compound interest. It took Dave a couple of years to convince Charlene—I said the women in our lives were strong, and strong-minded. I tend to think Charlene may have made up her mind sooner but was just checking out Dave's "mate traits." Sam, Bob, and I attended their wedding. Dave and Charlene recently celebrated their 51st anniversary. They have an accomplished forty-four-year-old daughter, Leah. Charlene and Sam's wife, Susan, were pregnant at the same time.

Dave's mom and my grandma *(Nonna)* were both single parents who raised healthy and successful children under difficult conditions. Each lost a mature child to an auto accident. *Nonna* had Neapolitan peasant toughness. She came over at fourteen years old, hearing impaired, and never really learned English. Her husband abandoned her with four children during the Depression. Her daughter, my Mamma Vina, eventually had to deal with the compulsive gambling of my biological father. He served federal prison time for imaginative ways of paying off his mob "creditors." Mamma left him for the sake of her two boys.

Dave was ten and his brother about eight when their mom divorced her husband, a USAF navigator. Dave recalls seeing his father only three times, but his mom was the soldier in the family. She was a doctor's receptionist/assistant across the street from their one-bedroom apartment over a garage. Rent, $25 a month, was exactly one week's wages. But she could be home when the boys got out of school, and she took advantage of a huge front lawn to teach them baseball. Not many people can say their mom threw lefty but batted right (just the opposite of Yogi Berra).

Dave's mom eventually bought a one-bath Cape (two blocks from the high school), then moved into an apartment, and finally into an assisted living facility of her own choosing. "She knew her own mind; if you made a suggestion and she said, 'I'll think about it,' you soon learned that idea was dead." Yes, she was another hard head. She lived to ninety-eight in October 2020.

Bob Hudak's Testimonial to His Strong Women. "My maternal grandmother, Francis Klein, was born in 1878 in Rochester, New York, to German immigrants. She attended school until the eighth grade, the usual educational limit for girls of the time. She worked in a shoe factory for the next ten years, saving her lunch money to buy books. Her collection included Burns, Browning, Emerson, Keats, Tennyson, Coleridge, Dickens, and of course, Shakespeare. She bought some; others were gifts. I have some of them, each inscribed as a gift or with just her name, always in pencil, on the inside cover, and dated with receipt date ranging from the mid-1890s through the early aughts.

"She somehow came to the attention of the superintendent of Rochester Public Schools. He encouraged her not to get a high school diploma, which she never did, but to take the University of Rochester entrance exam. She was admitted to the U of R in 1906 and graduated three years later magna cum laude and a member of Phi Beta Kappa at the age of thirty-one.

"She was a suffragette who lived just a few blocks from Susan B. Anthony. We do not know if they were acquainted. They were a generation apart but living a short walk from each other they must have had at least a passing acquaintance. After graduation, Francis Klein taught high school in Rochester where she met my grandfather, John Courtney, a student fourteen years her junior.

They were married in 1912. The Monroe County marriage record lists her occupation as 'teacher,' his as 'student.'

"Their daughter, Winifred Courtney, was my mother (b. 1918). She also attended the U of R where she met my father, Robert Hudak, first-generation Hungarian immigrant, and a promising optical engineer. Mom was a driving force in my life, and without her I probably would never have graduated from Cornell, such was my fear of disappointing her.

"I met my first wife, Gail, through Sam, who is her first cousin once removed; Sam's father and Gail's grandmother were siblings. We were married thirteen years, no children. Gail went on to earn her PhD in psychology after her liberation from me. We are still good friends and see each other on occasion.

"My wife, Patti, and I have been married thirty-three years and she (mostly) raised two strong and independent men of whom I'm very proud."

Joe's Testimonial to His Strong Women. My grandmother Nunziata, my mother, Vina, and my ex-wife, Mary, were strong women, and I hope I have made that case in Chapter Twenty-Five.

My partner, Nancy, has shown real strength and bravery. She was born in Uruguay "to Italian parents" as it said on her handwritten birth certificate. But, how could they know that her Ancestry.com report would identify her genome as more Italian than mine? She is a dreadnought combination of the muscular north and the vinegary, sinewy, hard-nosed south of survivors.

Nancy's husband died of cancer during her pregnancy to their third child. She struggled—for instance, by selling soap door-to-door—as she finished studies at the Vet School of the University of the Republic in Montevideo. She had serious run-ins with the military government that considered university personnel socialist enemies. Yet, she won a United Nations–sponsored fellowship to continue her studies abroad in animal reproductive biology, and she chose to do so at the University of Missouri, the home institution of a Fulbright Fellow, an American who was her mentor in Montevideo. Her three kids joined her soon after her Columbia, Missouri arrival.

Nancy stayed in Columbia, earning her Masters, and worked for a while in the animal sciences field. Eventually, she changed careers to one for which she still has real passion: teaching. At first, Nancy and I interacted in Latino causes and activities, such as serving on the board of the bilingual newspaper *Adelante*. Our boys played in the same local soccer leagues, and we often ran into each other at a weekly Latino dance event at Chevy's Fresh Mex. Chevy's atmosphere was almost that of a community square dance, three generations taking part and interacting. Hispanic heritage and fluency in Spanish were optional. Some local "blancos" were black belts in merengue and salsa. Music was by del Alma, a popular local *conjunto*.

Academic Achievement by "Our" Women. Our women were not only tough, they were also accomplished as mothers and in academia and professionally. A cumulative list of academic *bona fides* features three PhDs, three masters, a DVM, and an RN. Sam's, Susan and their daughter, Virginia, accompanied us on Chebeague Island and made everything go smoothly. Virginia and sister, Elizabeth, are Cornell alumnae. They became academic all-stars beyond their years on the Hill.

I emphasize that *all* the women with whom we shared our lives were competent as well as fantastic nurturers.

Interactions Over the Years. When fifty-five-plus years are compressed, the interactions among us four guys stand out. But only Sam visited my Brooklyn home. He wrote this account: "Lunch in Brooklyn in the back of your stepdad's store: Dandelion soup and whole artichokes. I had never seen either one before, although my grandmother had spoken of dandelion soup. I had no idea how to eat an artichoke and had to be shown how. I didn't finish my soup, not a meal easily forgotten."

The above passage, in juxtaposition with Sam's great-grandfather, Ezra, being jailed for violating the 1873 Comstock Act, makes me think of my great-grandparents back in the old country during the same era. What different lives my forebears led! They did not have time for causes any higher than gaining sustenance, as from roadside dandelions and artichokes that grew like the weeds they were.

Back in Bensonhurst, La Puma did not mention old-timers and their children scouring neighborhood vacant lots for edible weeds, such as cardoon (*gardune*), dandelions, and burdock. The harvest of edible weeds was still a practice in Bensonhurst well after Sal La Puma left for Westchester in 1959. Mushrooms were also part of the haul. By the way, cardoon is an East Coast artichoke (artichoke thistle, an invader from the Mediterranean, where else?), and its peeled stem is wonderful boiled and then deep-fried. I can imagine a few leafy stems, along with fig branches, secreted in the luggage at Ellis Island.

Coach Thoren (Chapter Seven) used to say "Polacco, you'd better shape up or you'll be selling pots and pans back on the streets of Naples." Would that there were such profitable trades "on the other side!"

Sam's impression of my store/home is so poignant:

"Brooklyn and the linoleum store were pretty much a cultural awakening, a truly urban experience. Sidwell Friends [Sam's Quaker prep school] and environs in northwest Washington, D.C. were very upscale. There was no subway, no overhead train, nor densely packed blocks after blocks. Then into the store: multiple rolls of linoleum standing on end like strange columns, and further back a table with food I'd never seen before with people I didn't know, some of whom didn't even speak English. It was good, all good. I had no idea what a privileged life I had been living." (Joe's note: Sam's appreciation of my youth really meant a lot to me—it was, well, validating.)

We Are Indeed a Tangled Web. I interacted with Sam and Hudak on the football field, and with Sam on that ill-advised hitch to Las Vegas, winter 1964 (Chapter Twelve). Of course, we four interacted socially, and on Chebeague we talked about the women of our undergraduate days, and beyond. When Sam returned to Cornell for his senior year, he roomed with Bob in an off-campus apartment. I was already at Duke, living with Mary, when we were visited by the Three Musketeers on at least one memorable occasion.

At our 2022 Maine reunion, Bob and Dave realized that they worked the same '60s summer in a Rochester meat (pork) processing plant. That was so long ago, a draft beer cost ten cents, and a pitcher a dollar. There was a foreshadowing of Dave's intelligence gathering when, by careful titration, he learned that the pitcher held only eight glasses, and he won his case with the tavern owner. We three guys attended Dave's marriage to Charlene, somewhere in the rural D.C. environs. The reception, catered by the ladies of the *Church of the Brethren*, was in a community recreation hall so that one of the punch bowls could be spiked with champaign. It seemed tame, but then again, so did my own wedding reception.

Sam, Dave, and Bob attended my 1968 wedding at a (Westport) Long Island Quaker Meeting House. (Mary's family was Quaker, and some nice Friends tried to broker a *dètente* between my future mother-in-law and me.) Then there was the reception back in Brooklyn (so my stepdad could attend), in the very Southern Italian Villa Vivolo. It was a relatively sedate affair, not the typical bashes of the Cotillion Terrace (or La Puma's Paradise Ballroom) with live music, dancing, flying sandwiches, and *paesani* emulating Dean Martin and Louis Prima. (The food of the Villa, though, was fantastic and gained fame when news broke of the police break-up of a mob "sit-down" there.) Mary and I made off that night (New Year's Eve, 1968) for Durham, exiting off the Jersey Turnpike for our honeymoon. We were already a family, as we secreted Carmine "Squirrel Monkey" Polacco into the motel room.

The Boys-to-(Old) Men. Sam, my transcontinental traveling buddy, my savior in the Rockies (Chapter Twelve), returned to Cornell where he kicked academic butt, and then attended the Medical College of Virginia, a part of Virginia Commonwealth University in Richmond. Mary and I and our three kids visited Sam and Susan in Shawsville, Virginia, and later in Johnstown, Pennsylvania. Sam continued his practice in family medicine in Tuscaloosa, Alabama, and ran their residency program. He is now professor emeritus at the University of Alabama. I can devote a lot of ink to Sam's successful career, but Susan's nursing and public health creds are more impressive, and her published work has higher citation ratings. (I am citing Sam here.)

Bob, my little brother in our Cornell fraternity got through a rocky academic career with eyes fixed on unconventional career goals. I believe he found his college courses unchallenging, and therefore boring. His business has been as successful as it is unconventional, providing (OK, selling) organic plant biostimulants to growers of all kinds of crops in varied climactic zones worldwide. If this sounds like botanical snake oil, it is not. His customers are as faithful as they are successful. And Bob can give the physiological reasons (or reasonable facsimiles) why his emollients work. In Maine, I overheard his pro bono advice to some members of his large extended clientele family.

And I'm very impressed that Bob actually does field trials.

Dave was the only nonathlete of our group, at least by the criterion of playing on an intercollegiate team. He went his own way to the CIA, which he left twenty years ago. I believe he was an early assessor/predictor of grain yields in the Soviet Union by Landsat, and later by digital satellite imaging. As a scientist, I appreciate the accumulation of accurate and extensive data, and in the role of data collection I support *the company*. Would that we had better intelligence at critical times in our recent history (duhhh). Dave is a repository of stories and insights. He rose to the highest non–politically appointed position (executive director, or "Number 3") and was "responsible for everything, from strategic planning to making sure the waste baskets are emptied [. . .] To say I'm still working is technically correct, but I 'do' board of directors so it's not an everyday deal and certainly less 'work' than what Bob must go through."

I will not bore the reader with the shifting matrix of our shared living arrangements during and shortly after Cornell. Amazingly, or not, some fifty-plus years after college graduation we four have arrived at congruent opinions, on politics, life, and environmental issues (and depressing conclusions). We are family men, three of us grandfathers. (Bob just joined the club and Dave has more than one grandpuppy.) But I think the key to being ensconced in manhood is that we married women of substance and achievement.

New England is often thought of as the territory of those flinty Yankees, those stubborn taciturn settlers who put down deep and permanent roots in the rocky soil. I'm sure they're out there, but on the night celebrating my 78th birthday, our restaurant hosted a rousing Jewish wedding celebration. What a country.

Our three or four days together did not constitute an anticipatory mourning of our close-to-closing life cycles. Yes, we knew the curtain was primed to fall, but who cared? We were in the here-and-now and very much enjoying it. Sam's Susan took a picture of four old guys, regally seated on a hillcrest, a golden tribunal gazing toward the setting sun. Our *Four Seasons* were now down to one golden penumbra, witnessed by the high priests of Ra. Bob titled the photo: "Four old men gazing into the sunset of their lives." Hey, Bob, youngster, we had a great view; we were relaxed and grateful for each other's company.

So, what does all this have to do with Don Salvatore La Puma? Sal and I shared the Bensonhurst launch pad, from which I was sent into orbit and rendezvoused with fellow travelers Bob, Sam, and Dave. At the tender age of thirty, Don Salvatore moved to Westchester as an advertising copyeditor, and seven years after that he relocated to Santa Barbara. Sal and I both looked back at Bensonhurst. I know Sal did 'cause *The Boys of Bensonhurst* came out thirty-two years after his move to California.

You can take the boys out of the 'hood, but make sure they're accompanied by strong women.

The view, and each other's
company, were beautiful
and reinforcing.

Jerome Lester Horwitz, **Curly of "Three Stooges"** fame, was on the Bensonhurst Junior High School 128 basketball team.

EPILOGUE

A Sixtieth High School Reunion

(June 2022, NY City)

We're thankful to have made it this far.
And to look way back, with no cold malaise
We're not here to write a memoir
Just party and jive, like old compadres

That goes for all but a very few (well, one)
Who seemed to resent his life's fate
For it was not he who had well won
The accolades to prove he was so great

Stuyvesant HS class of 1962 reunion editor, Stan Mandel, asked me to write a "light" 500-word bio for our reunion volume. So, this lighthearted (OK, lightweight) bio follows, though my anagrammarian soul finds a disturbing similarity between bio and obit.

I was born in Bensonhurst, and attended its public schools before crossing the East River to attend Stuyvesant. But I am indebted to PS 101 and Bensonhurst Junior High School 128, short-term alma *matres* of Moe and Jerome Lester Howard (nè Horwitz) of the Three Stooges. Their ghosts oft confused my better judgment, and sense of reality. For instance, I thought mob intervention might have placed me on the Stuyvesant "accept" list. All this is moot since virtually all the old wise guys are gone, giving me a reprieve from returning any favors—real, imagined or claimed.

I must also acknowledge Ms. Brady, a very authoritarian ninth grade Social Studies teacher. In military cadence, she informed me that I was accepted by Stuyvesant, and that I *would* attend.

Her marching order was key. I was fully expecting to take over my father's linoleum store after Lafayette HS. However, with my Stuyvesant diploma in hand, I was pushed to Cornell (BS in biochemistry, 1966) and Duke (PhD in biochemistry and genetics, 1971). But, you can't take the boy completely out of Bensonhurst . . . I took a road less-travelled and became an assistant professor of biochemistry at the Universidad del Valle in Cali, Colombia (where I put Stuyvesant baseball skills to some dubious use [Chapter Eighteen]). In 1974, I was drawn away from Cali to postdoc at Brookhaven National Laboratories with enlightened plant geneticist, the late Peter S. Carlson, who believed science should more directly address human needs, an attitude I picked up in Colombia. Nine months later, I became a staff geneticist at New Haven's Connecticut Agricultural Experiment Station (CAES), by happy coincidence close to Bensonhurst.

You can take the boy out of Bensonhurst, but . . . frustrations with the CAES administration brought out my *enfant terrible* nature. Somehow, five years later (1979), I had accomplished enough to garner the positive attention of the Biochemistry Department of the University of Missouri (MU).

I was happy to become part of MU's internationally respected Interdisciplinary Plant Group. And my academic career has had an international flavor. To my Stuyvesant classmates: show me spawning waters more international than those of Bensonhurst. After my stint as Assistant Professor in the Biochemistry Section of the Universidad del Valle Med School (Cali, Colombia, 1972/1973), I became a Fulbright Fellow in Spain (2000/1) and Argentina (2005), a visiting professor in Brazil (at the Federal University in Porto Alegre, 2008/2009, and three months at the Luiz de Queiroz College of Agriculture, University of São Paulo, 2011.) I was active in MU-Mexico (Universidad Nacional Autónoma de México) interactions in training plant scientists. Research/teaching collaborations also extended to Costa Rica, Germany and Italy.

I have taught in Argentina, Brazil, Colombia, Costa Rica, and Argentina, and given seminars in several countries, often in Spanish or Portuguese (or broken Italian in Bari and Pisa).

Blah Blah Blah: My CV lists peer-reviewed research articles, reviews, opinion pieces, book chapters, monographs, etc., and I will not bore Stuyvesant classmates with numbers. (So who's counting, already?) I *am* proud, though, that my MU lab was at times bilingual, and that gringos learned the Spanish for "where's the large funnel?" (*¿Dónde está el embudo grande?*)

At MU I taught undergraduate, graduate, and medical students and introduced biotech outreach courses to non-majors.

In retirement, I write mostly non (but *not* anti-) science, including real and faux poetry, and am invited to recite at MU events honoring/roasting students and faculty. See "About the Author" for Joe's non-science output.

I ask my classmates' indulgence as I extend two special personal greetings to Stuyvesant luminaries:

Dear Coach Thrush: You, Murl, were a great influence. Folks back in Missouri would not believe that a Midwest footballer made a living coaching high school football among the tenements of lower Manhattan. Yet, Coach, you prepared me to be an All-American lightweight football player at Cornell. I'm sure this did not get into your *résumé*. The NFL—even the upstart AFL—passed over this 165-pound offensive tackle—*da noiv*. You built people, Coach, not draft choices.

Dear Ms. Perucci: I should have cut a few football practices to take Advanced Math. My answer to "Are you planning to play professional football?" was clearly "no." Cerebral shortcomings in class scared me more than potential brain damage on the gridiron.

Ms. Perrucci, I don't know where I first heard the truism: *We are the people we were in high school.* Classmates I came across at the reunion confirmed that the ceramic that filled our high school molds is now, sixty years later, more firmly set, well, like Portland Cement. Call us PC, Perucci's Children grown up to obstinate boyhood. Take it from this *capo dosto*.

Finally, Dear Classmates: I am waiting in LaGuardia to return to Missouri, after having reminisced about Bensonhurst, my four immigrant grandparents, and my youthful intemperance. Before I board the St. Louis plane, one last Bensonhurst perspective, by a famous St. Louis native:

"We shall not cease from exploration
And the end of all our exploring
Will be to arrive where we started
And know the place for the first time."

—T.S. Eliot, 1943, from "Little Gidding,"
Four Quartets

Was this Sal La Puma's realization when he composed *The Boys of Bensonhurst* while living in Santa Barbara, California?

> 66 *I recall summer Tuesdays when there was the sound of shelling over Coney Island Beach and Gravesend Bay—not to fear, it was Schaefer Beer's summer fireworks spectacular, all the better to watch the submarine races.* 99

—Joe Polacco,
University of Missouri
Emeritus Prof. of
Biochemistry

ABOUT THE AUTHOR

(https://josephpolacco.me)

Joe Polacco is a native of Brooklyn's Bensonhurst neighborhood and a product of NYC public schools including Manhattan's Stuyvesant High School. He earned a bachelor's degree in biochemistry from Cornell in 1966, and a doctorate in biochemistry and genetics from Duke in 1971. Joe is currently Professor Emeritus of Biochemistry at the University of Missouri.

It is not fully appreciated that all scientists write, a lot. Joe has written MANY research proposals which were cast down to a shredded paper (or a digital) void, but some proposals were elevated enough to bring financial support to Joe's research program. As a result, Joe and colleagues authored research papers, book chapters, reviews, patents and edited monographs. More importantly, they have made contributions to understanding plant nitrogen and mineral metabolism and plant interactions with bacteria. Joe's teaching has been recognized—mostly in a positive light.

Joe was awarded Senior Fulbright Fellowships in Spain and Argentina, and two visiting professorships in Brazil.

Joe lives with Nancy Malugani in Columbia, Missouri. Six children live in California, Florida, Virginia, and Uruguay amid a miasma of nine grandchildren.

"Ruby June," Sheep Dog/Black Lab mix, and feline mutt "Jasman" complete the gang.

Also by Joe:
Vina, A Brooklyn Memoir
Giovanni, Street Urchin of Naples
    (Historical fiction novel)
A Life's Rambles/Ramblas de una Vida
    (Bilingual English-Spanish rhyming verse)

TONGUE-IN-CHEEK

66 *Bensonhurst Manifest Destiny: OK, so Bensonhurst is not Bay Ridge or Bath Beach, but we can claim those areas whose borders we share, just as Balboa who, upon sighting the Pacific, claimed the ocean and all the lands it touched for Spain.* 99

—Joe Polacco,
Bensonhurst's
Rocky Balboa

255

Tongue-in-cheek? How about that Bensonhurst home whose frontage, complete with lane dividers, is the neighborhood wax museum? That's the way it is, now. The way it was—a last longing look at my Bensonhurst immigrant microcosm just around my corner.

Bay 31st Street, 1960: Brother Michael at 13 with Eddie Odland (left) and Tommie Capelli (page 257), sons of the Emerald Isle and Sicily. In need of a seat never overlook a trashcan. Our 86th Street home/store (*Greg's Floor Covering, Inc.*) was around the corner. Eddie, Tommie and Michael represented distinct ingredients in the Bensonhurst immigrant minestrone. The cans were between Ludemann's corner *Ice Cream Parlor* and *Longo Shoe Repair.* Irascible Mr. Longo considered shoes that needed repair a personal affront. With his *de Nobili* stogie hanging by spit from his lower lip he'd cast our needy shoes on a work pile

while uttering Old World blasphemies. (The shoes always came back beautifully redeemed.)

Ludemann's widow lived upstairs—a very sweet German lady with an accent. On summer evenings, she'd sit outside her staircase near the garbage cans, sometimes engaging Mr. Longo in conversation. And then, sweetness happened, a loving relationship developed. Longo's was right next to the Spadaro house which to me was a mansion—so beautifully was it remodeled with immigrant labor.

Across Bay 31st: *Wing-Lee* (Chinese) *Laundry* and (Italian) *Joe's Barbershop*. Michael pointed out that pioneering psychedelic artist, Peter Max, once lived over *Wing-Lee* with his parents, the immigrant Finkelsteins—such exotic immigrant interactions. Walk to the corner and look right on 86th Street, toward the "Taj Mahal" bank on 23rd Avenue (page vi). The Bank and Vinnie (page ix) guarded the flanks of that hallowed stretch, the wondrous casbah that greeted me each morning, and sang me to sleep at night.

ACKNOWLEDGMENTS

Thanks to fellow travelers, even the anonymous strangers who made the journey "interesting." A joy in composing this "confessional retrospective" was re-connecting with Morgan, Kelly Woodbury, my brother, Michael Grandé Polacco, Stuyvesant HS Class of 1962 mates and teammates, and those three old men on Chebeague Island: Sam Gaskins, Bob Hudak and Dave Carey. Oh, *meine (Wilhelmina?)* Billie Schildkraut, from Cornell to Cofradia, Honduras to the Brooklyn Cyclones in Coney Island— what a beautiful fellow traveler; and José (Don Chepito) Ayala, to Honduras with our love for you, Rosa and family. Petey Thumbs LaMontia: you convinced me I wasn't daft—our memories actually jibed. Even if we mutually molded them to the best possible shape, all the more reason to thank you. *Cugina* Toni Caggiano, your accurate recall of the old 'hood was essential.

The Columbia Writers' Guild, the Universalist Unitarian writers' group, and lovely beta readers, thanks to you all—Frank Montagnino, Deb Sutton and more. Fran Reynolds, oh Fran. We met on a supermarket checkout line, where you thanked me for opening up to Mizzou's Korean students. Since then, you were both a fan and a constructive critic. Dang it, I miss you.

Poetry? Moi? In Bensonhurstese: *I couldn'ta done it widoutya:* Sharon SingingMoon, Barb Leonhard, Melinda "Food Sleuth" Hemmelgarn, Jane Frazier, Shirley Seabaugh, David Tager. Tomorrow I will remember another "army" that came to my rescue.

Melody Kroll, your camera brought out the best in my author photo. Would that it could do the same for my writing. Katherine Pickett (POP Editing): THANKS. Folks at Barringer: Jeff Schlesinger, baseball fan par excellence, and always in the literary on-deck circle. Linda Duider dealt with unreasonable formatting ideas, and yet came through with beautifully bedazzling cover design and layout. Your initials are rightly LSD.

My thanks to Jim and Rosalie Mangano, here on a Grand Street bench after a sumptuous Chinese meal in polyglot lower Manhattan.

Polyglot? Jim and Rosalie can order (and cook) in Sicilian, Chinese, Japanese and in the important culinary terminology of other languages. And, that is not tongue in cheek, unless it's on the menu.

Rojim: though my immigrant "memory" wanes, you helped me retrieve so much from the old days.

CPSIA information can be obtained
at www.ICGtesting.com
Printed in the USA
JSHW010949260723
45407JS00002B/10